Internet for Teachers & Parents

Illustrator:
Wendy Chang

Editor:
Evan D. Forbes, M.S. Ed.

Editor in Chief:
Sharon Coan, M.S. Ed.

Art Director:
Elayne Roberts

Associate Designer:
Denise Bauer

Production Manager:
Phil Garcia

Imaging:
Alfred Lau
James Edward Grace

Trademarks:
Trademarked names and graphics appear throughout this book. Instead of listing every firm and entity which owns the trademarks or inserting a trademark symbol with each mention of a trademarked name, the publisher avers that it is using the names and graphics only for editorial purposes and to the benefit of the trademarked owner with no intention of infringing upon that trademark.

Publishers:
Rachelle Cracchiolo, M.S. Ed.
Mary Dupuy Smith, M.S. Ed.

Author:

Paul Gardner

Teacher Created Materials, Inc.
6421 Industry Way
Westminster, CA 92683
www.teachercreated.com
ISBN-1-55734-668-2
©1996 Teacher Created Materials, Inc.
Revised, 1999
Made in U.S.A.

TABLE OF CONTENTS

INTRODUCTION

Welcome to the wonderful world of the Internet, a vast expanse of information and communication, the freedom of which has not been seen in the history of the world. It is now possible for one to find information on nearly any topic at the touch of a finger upon a keyboard or mouse. Unlike the printed medium, a computer attached to the Internet is not limited to text and pictures. Today's information superhighway is alive with sound, video, and animation. Written correspondence that once took days to be delivered can now be read within seconds after being sent. Even face to face video conferencing with people all over the world can be done if one has the right hardware and software.

If you think you will not be part of this change, look at history. The telegraph, telephone, and television were all considered luxury items at one time and not one of these inventions has grown in popularity at the rate that the Internet has. In fact, the global telecommunication network called the Internet is just the technological evolution of the three aforementioned inventions.

In the face of such a radical change in how we get our information, we must educate ourselves, our children, and our students that it is the information and not the Internet that is important. Students must learn not only how to find the information but to process it, evaluate it, and use it in a responsible manner.

The next five decades will create a paradigm shift in the way we and our schools relate to the world. The information superhighway has become a reality. From your school, office, or home you will be able to travel all over the world to gather and share information, interact with others, and take part in discussions and adventures. As more people travel this electronic highway, maps to find information and rules to keep traveling safe become vital to successfully completing the journey.

HOW TO USE THIS BOOK

Internet for Teachers and Parents has been designed to be an easy-to-use reference for teaching and learning on and with the Internet. Depending upon your level of Internet experience, you may refer to this book often or just on occassion. Whatever the case may be, it is available as a resource to you as you integrate the use of the Internet into your classroom or family plan.

The book is divided into eight sections:

- **What Is the Internet?**
- **Netiquette and Nethics**
- **Safe Surfing**
- **Connecting to the Internet**
- **Internet Tools**
- **Integrating the Internet into the Curriculum**
- **Lesson Plans**
- **Internet Resources**

There is also a general glossary of terms, a section on where and how to get funding for using the Internet, an index and a bibliography containing books in print about the Internet, as well as live Internet sites you can explore.

Your present knowledge of the Internet will determine where you should start reading this book. If you have never surfed on the Internet and only thought surfing was something you did in the ocean, then it is suggested that you start at the beginning. If you consider yourself a Web surfer, then use this book as a resource to take you places you haven't been before. If you are somewhere in between, then figure out what you don't know and find that section in the book. Everything you need to know to surf and use the Internet is here at your finger tips. All you need is access to a computer, modem, and the desire to learn and have fun.

Note: At the time of this printing all Web sites were accurate. Teacher Created Materials attempts to offset the fickle nature of the Web by posting changes of URLs on our Web site. Check our home page at www.teachercreated.com for updates on this book.

WHAT IS THE INTERNET?

TELECOMMUNICATIONS

You cannot begin a discussion of the Internet without understanding telecommunications. It is the ability for computers to exchange information over distance. This is usually done with a piece of hardware called a modem. Modems translate the digital information that a computer uses into analog, or sound information, that can be transmitted over telephone lines. Once transmitted, a computer equipped with a modem at the other end of the line receives the analog information and translates it back to its digital form. Computers can use this "connectivity" to exchange documents, programs, or mail and even control each other.

WHAT IS A NETWORK?

Maybe you have gotten together with others "to network." This trendy term, meaning to get together with other people to exchange ideas or information, was actually derived from the computer term "network." A computer network is any two or more computers that are linked so that they can communicate with each other. Networks are usually "hard-wired," meaning they do not need modems to communicate. A local area network (LAN) is the connection of computers at a common site, like a school or business. These LANs can be attached to a wide area network (WAN) like a district or county network. Many school districts are attaching their networks to the Internet.

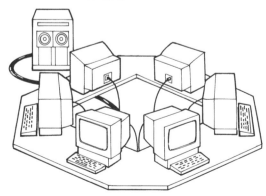

WHAT IS THE INTERNET? *(cont.)*

The Internet is the "network of networks." It is a global technology network made up of many smaller contributing networks. They all speak the same language called Internet protocol or IP. This system gives immediate access to information. It is like being able to open any book in any library from your computer. You can look at and print articles, documents, and pictures, as well as review current facts about news, weather, and sports that you may use in your classes. However, the Internet is not merely a library, this tool also makes it possible for users to communicate through electronic mail (e-mail), in real time on chat lines, or even through video conferencing.

The Internet was created in 1983 with 100 networks and has grown by leaps and bounds. By 1993, there were approximately 10,000 networks attached to the Internet. Most experts believe the amount of networks currently attached to the Internet is in the millions. Since each of the connected networks can be as many as tens of thousands of computers, the total number of individual users of the Internet is most likely in the tens of millions worldwide.

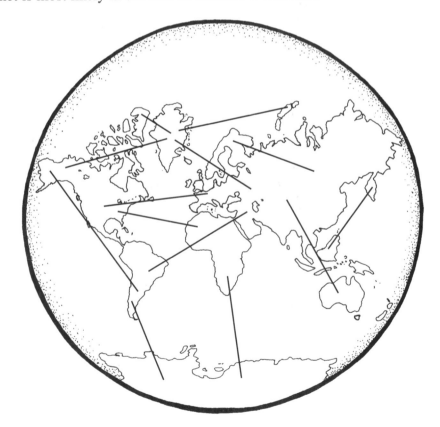

WHAT IS THE INTERNET? *(cont.)*

WHY SHOULD I USE THE INTERNET IN THE CLASSROOM?

The Internet gives teachers, parents, and students access to information of a quality and quantity never before seen in education. Using the Internet allows the user to retrieve information, media, and even software from all over the world almost instantly. This allows students, teachers, parents, or anyone using this tool to have this valuable information for individual or cooperative projects.

But gathering information is merely one aspect of the power of the Internet—communication is the other. Once you have access to the Internet, you have access to all the users of the Internet—teachers sharing and collaborating with other teachers, students with other students, scientists and business people, everyone. Distance, class, race, and culture are no longer barriers to the sharing of ideas. People can simply communicate.

Some uses of the Internet include, but are not limited to, the following:

- gathering information on almost any subject
- communicating with others via e-mail
- joining discussion groups on a specific topic
- publishing student work
- communicating with experts in any field
- taking part in electronic expeditions

WHAT IS THE INTERNET? *(cont.)*

WHAT CAN YOU DO WITH THE INTERNET?

No, it won't make julienne fries, but if it's information and communication you want, a better question might be, "What can't the Internet do?" Most functions of the Internet fall into these following families:

- **Electronic Mail (e-mail):** Corresponding electronically with people who are connected to the "Net".

- **Usenet Newsgroups:** A worldwide bulletin board service divided into interests. You "post" messages and others "post" replies.

- **Mailing Lists:** E-mail lists divided by interests. You send e-mail to interest groups and they reply.

- **TELNET:** Logging on to and using a computer from a remote location.

- **File Transfer Protocol (FTP):** Transferring files like software and documents from one computer to another.

- **Chat:** Engaging in discussions with others simply by typing.

- **World Wide Web (WWW):** Gathering information through the use of the new graphic information system.

Don't let this list scare you. In the past you would have needed separate pieces of software and/or long strings of commands to carry out any one of these functions. With today's graphical Internet interface software (fancy language for point and click), all of these functions can be done using one program. Sometimes you won't even realize that you are doing them.

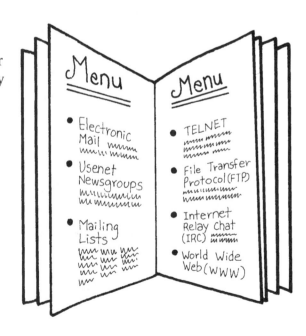

NETIQUETTE AND NETHICS

THE RULES OF THE INFORMATION SUPERHIGHWAY

Before we get started with our road trip down the information superhighway, it is important to know the rules of the road.

From the *Concise Oxford Dictionary*

Etiquette: n. conventional rules of personal behavior in polite society

Ethic[s]: n. 1. a. relating to morals, treating of moral questions; morally correct; honorable

Just as there are behaviors which are acceptable at school, students need to learn the correct procedures and rules for using the Internet. Netiquette, the etiquette of the Net, and Nethics, the ethics of the Net, are the rules of the information superhighway.

Before beginning to use these exciting communication and research tools, it is important to understand the many consequences of the new computer connections that will be made. This powerful educational tool is a privilege. It can provide countless hours of exploration and use, but like a drivers license, it is a privilege that can be taken away for breaking the rules.

NETIQUETTE AND NETHICS *(cont.)*

The following is a list of helpful rules when using the Internet:

You're Not Dealing with Computers, You're Dealing with People

Sending a message that is strongly critical is called a "flame." To avoid "flaming," never say anything to someone that you would not say to them in person. Avoid the use of sarcasm and be careful with humor. Without voice inflections and body language, remarks can be misinterpreted.

Do Not Post Personal Information About Anyone

The Internet is becoming a very crowded place. Like society as a whole, there are nice people and there are not-so-nice people. Do not give out your home phone number or your address to anyone.

Be Brief

More people will read your information if it is short and clear. This also helps conserve disk space on computers.

Do Not Harass Users

If someone asks that you not contact them, you must stop **all** contact immediately. You may feel you have the right to freedom of expression, but others have the right to be free from harassment.

Be Careful of Copyrights

Cut and paste functions make electronic media extremely easy to use when communicating one's own, as well as others' ideas. As long as you are using an article for educational purposes and not selling it, you may use the information. It is important, however, to cite all references.

Double Check Downloads

There are many software products available on the Internet. Many of these products are offered free of charge. Be sure the software product you are downloading is not a commercial product that has been distributed illegally.

Give Credit Where Credit Is Due

Remember, the work that someone has placed on the Internet is free for you to use, but if you do use it, give the writer or creator credit.

NETIQUETTE AND NETHICS *(cont.)*

THE TEN COMMANDMENTS FOR COMPUTER ETHICS (NETHICS) FROM THE COMPUTER ETHICS INSTITUTE

1. Thou shalt not use a computer to harm other people.
2. Thou shalt not interfere with other people's computer work.
3. Thou shalt not snoop around in other people's files.
4. Thou shalt not use a computer to steal.
5. Thou shalt not use a computer to bear false witness.
6. Thou shalt not use or copy software for which you have not paid.
7. Thou shalt not use other people's computer resources without authorization.
8. Thou shalt not appropriate other people's intellectual output.
9. Thou shalt think about the social consequences of the program you write.
10. Thou shalt use a computer in ways that show consideration and respect.

SAFE SURFING

RULES FOR SAFE SURFING

Because the Internet is public domain, free speech is not only the right, but the rule. Therefore, nearly anyone can publish nearly anything on it. We must acknowledge the fact that there are inappropriate materials on the Internet and then do everything we can to actively avoid them. We cannot weed out all of the materials that are unacceptable for academic purposes, but it should be clearly understood by all students that access to such material in any form is strictly forbidden.

In order to make the responsibility of using this tool clear, many educational institutions have developed Acceptable Use Plans or AUPs. These AUPs usually include a contract that is quite clear about the responsibilities of the student and must be signed by the student, as well as their parents or guardians. To find examples of AUPs see ERIC Online: http://eric.syr.edu

Although the actual percentage of unacceptable materials is small, it is a cause for concern for students, parents, and teachers. If a student stumbles onto the information while doing legitimate research, he/she should contact the teacher or person responsible for technology at school.

There is no fool proof way of keeping students out of areas where they should not be. Here are a few general rules of thumb when students are surfing the net:

- Supervision, Supervision, Supervision. Keep an eye on students while they are using the Internet.
- Send an agreement home for parents to sign that explains the benefits and risks of Internet research.
- Make students aware of "Netiquette"—the rules of using the Internet. (See page 11.)
- Create a list of Internet sites that are safe. Require that your students visit only those areas.
- Create your own homepage with safe surfing sites on it. These directories can be customized with links to Internet sites that are proven safe and educationally sound.
- Use one of the net monitoring programs that are available to block out inappropriate information. (See page 13.)
- Parents: Spend some family time netsurfing. There are plenty of sites that provide excellent material.

The Internet can be an educational gold mine of information, not only for your students but for you as well. It is the way people will receive most of their information in the future. With a few precautions, teachers and students can reap the benefits of this vast network of information.

SAFE SURFING *(cont.)*

SOME NET MONITORING SOFTWARE

There are several products on the market that help block inappropriate information from crossing the screen of minors. A few of the more popular are shown below. All of these can be downloaded (a copy moved from their computer to yours) in demonstration form. Most demos will work for a month and then disable themselves.

Name: *Cyber Patrol*

Company's Product Description: *Cyber Patrol* is used to manage Internet access, limit the total time spent online, and block access to Internet sites that you deem inappropriate.

Download demonstration copy at: http://www.cyberpatrol.com/

Name: *Net Nanny*

Company's Product Description: *Net Nanny* is the only software program that allows YOU to monitor, screen, and block access to anything residing on, running in, out, or through your PC, online or off.

Download demonstration copy at: http://www.netnanny.com/

Name: *SurfWatch*

Company's Product Description: *SurfWatch* blocks tens of thousands of explicit sites locally at the user's machine, without restricting the access rights of other Internet users, and without removing any material from the Internet or any server.

Download demonstration copy at: http://www.surfwatch.com/

GUIDELINES FOR PUBLISHING WORK ON THE INTERNET

The fantastic thing about the Internet is that it can be a global audience for children's work. There are several Internet sites listed in the back of this book that allow students to post projects. These sometimes allow kids to post a photo of themselves with their work. Before you attempt this you should have a signed release from parents. A sample release is provided for you on page 14. If you are involved with a school district, check to see if they have a procedure in place for this type of thing. If not, have them check over the release before using it.

SAFE SURFING *(cont.)*

RELEASE FOR ELECTRONICALLY DISPLAYED STUDENT WORK

Dear Parents/Guardians,

We are excited to let you know that our class will be publishing our work on a portion of the Internet called the World Wide Web. This means that anyone in the world who has access to the Web will be able to view your child's work. The potential audience is in the millions.

Your signature below acknowledges permission for such work to be published on the World Wide Web.

Yours truly,

Classroom Teacher

☐ My child's work, which may be accompanied by his/her first name, may be electronically displayed and produced.

☐ My child's work, which may not be accompanied by his/her first name, may be electronically displayed and produced.

☐ Photographs of my child, which may be accompanied by his/her first name, may be electronically displayed and produced.

☐ Photographs of my child, which may not be accompanied by his/her first name, may be electronically displayed and produced.

I hereby give the above permission and release_____ from any liability resulting from or connected with the publication of such work.

_____
Child's Name

_____
Teacher

_____
Parent or Guardian Signature

_____
Date

CONNECTING TO THE INTERNET

WHAT DO I NEED TO GET CONNECTED?

Other than a computer there are only a couple of things that are needed to connect to the Internet.

Modem

Computers speak and understand digital language. Telephone lines carry what is called analog information. This is like trying to communicate with someone who speaks another language. A modem facilitates the communication by becoming an interpreter. Modems translate digital information to analog and analog to digital, acting as an interface between the computer and the phone line.

Like a good interpreter, good modems are fast and accurate. When purchasing a modem be aware of its speed. Modem speed is expressed in BPS or bits per second. Early modems transmitted 300 bits per minute. Due to the graphic nature of the Internet, these modems might take from several minutes to several hours to translate the information it takes to display a page of text or graphics. Today modems are much faster. Most modems translate at 28.8 Kbps or 28,000 BPS or faster. When purchasing a modem, buy the fastest that you can afford because if it is not convenient to use the Internet's resources, there is no need to be connected.

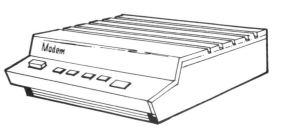

A Telephone Line

Your normal telephone line will work fine for connecting to the Internet. Be aware though that while you are online the telephone will be busy. Many people who use the Internet frequently add a separate telephone line for data and fax. Even features like call waiting must be turned off during connection time in order not to corrupt the incoming data. Check with your phone company on how to temporarily disable these types of services.

Some phone companies offer other services like high speed digital systems, but these are usually too expensive for home use. These systems also require other types of hardware like network cards. Many schools have begun to make these connections with help from grant funds and special state and local projects.

CONNECTING TO THE INTERNET *(cont.)*

A SERVICE PROVIDER

There are several companies that can get you connected to the Internet. They are divided into two distinctive groups—Commercial Online Services (COS) and Internet Service Providers (ISP). Commercial Online Services usually provide a range of services within their own network, as well as giving you access to the Internet. Internet Service Providers (ISP) provide no other services than e-mail and access to the Internet. Some of these services are listed in the tables below.

This table explains the differences between an Internet Service Provider and a Commercial Online Service.

	Commercial Online Service	Internet Service Provider
User Interface	usually better	only as good as your software
Added services	yes	sometimes
Cost	several plans	usually a flat rate
Security	some added features	seperate software usually required
Support	yes	yes
Access speed	slow in some areas	usually high speed
Choice of browsers	limited	any browser

COMMERCIAL ONLINE SERVICES

Name	Phone Number
America Online (AOL)	800-827-6364
CompuServe	800-848-8990
Prodigy	800-776-3449
Microsoft Network	800-386-5550

CONNECTING TO THE INTERNET *(cont.)*

INTERNET SERVICE PROVIDERS

Name	Phone Number
Earthlink Total Access	800-395-8410
NetCom	800-638-2661

The Internet Service Providers listed above are some who have national access through toll free and local phone numbers. Many smaller local companies provide great service. Check your yellow pages under Internet Service Providers for a list of companies that provide this service.

Software

You will need a software package to connect and then to view and navigate the Internet. Today most all of the software you need is provided in one software package. For example, browser software like *Netscape* (Netscape Communications) and *Internet Explorer* (Microsoft) both integrate most all the software you need to use the Internet.

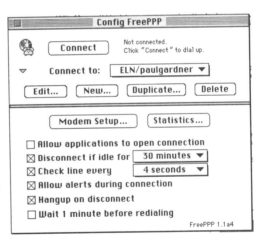

Many ISPs will provide you with browser software, SLIP (Serial Line Internet Protocol) or PPP (Point to Point Protocol), when you join their service. SLIP and PPP software are the programs that tell your computer to connect with the network. Their sole purpose is to get you connected. Once connected, the browser takes over and does all the work.

Commercial Online Services usually will require you to use their software, which is free. Many of these services are converting to allow their customers to use other browsers.

CONNECTING TO THE INTERNET *(cont.)*

WHAT ABOUT THE COMPUTER?

The rules of thumb for buying a computer for Internet access are like that for buying a computer for any other use. Get as much as you can for the money that you want to spend. Here is what is meant.

Platform

Platform refers to the type of computer/operating system that you require. There are two major choices: Windows or Macintosh (DOS ships standard on all IBMs and compatibles). In the past this was a major decision in that IBM and compatible machines could not run Macintosh programs and visa-versa. With the development of software translators and dual platforms (run both) machines, the problems have become less significant. However, this is still a consideration. Here are a few questions that will help you or your school make the platform decision.

1. What platform do people who you share documents with most often use? If only one, choose that platform. If both, choose a platform that can easily operate in both environments.

2. What platform offers the software which you use or are interested in using? Most companies produce software versions for both platforms, however, because of the abundance of IBM compatibles, you will usually find them more accessible through retailers. Macintosh software, although also available through retailers, tends to be easier to get through mail order sources like Mac Mall, Mac Warehouse, and educational suppliers.

Processor

The brain of any computer is its microprocessor. The ability to handle large computing jobs with speed and accuracy depends largely on the microprocessor. Computer manufacturers have evolved through several microprocessors, each generation more fleet and powerful than the last. Compare the speed of the microprocessor with other models in your price range. The computing speed of a microprocessor is listed in megahertz or MHz.

RAM

Random Access Memory or RAM is the computer's short-term memory—the memory that it needs to carry out a program's instructions. As software becomes more and more memory intensive, it is important to buy a computer with enough RAM to handle it. RAM's unit of measure is the megabyte or MB. Here are a few questions to ask:

1. How much RAM does the operating system software use? Windows and MacOS require a large amount of RAM just to run the computer.

2. What types of programs am I going to run? Most graphic interfaces require a large amount of RAM. Look at the backs of software packages that you are interested in and check the minimum RAM requirements, then add at least 25% more as a safety net.

CONNECTING TO THE INTERNET *(cont.)*

3. Will you run more than one program at a time? If you are a first time computer user you may not think that you will; however, the time savings of being able to move information from one program to another is extremely useful—like when your students are writing reports and they need pictures or text from the Internet. If so, add the minimum memory requirements for both programs and the system together and add 25% for safety.

4. Is the RAM easily upgradable and what is the maximum RAM upgradability? As computer programs are developed that require more memory, it is important that you are able to "keep up."

Storage

Storage is the amount of long-term memory that a computer can file or store. There are several storage devices on the market. Like RAM, storage is also measured in megabytes (MB) or gigabytes (GB). There are 1,000 megabytes in a gigabyte. Almost all computers now come with an internal hard disk drive and at least one removable disk drive. Both of these would be considered storage.

You should make sure to make back-up copies of all important documents and programs on something other than your hard disk. Even with the reliability of hard disks these days, stuff happens!

Monitor

With the graphic and increasingly multimedia environment that exists on the World Wide Web, it is important to have a monitor and computer that support full color. If you are to take advantage of the multimedia (text, sound, animation, video, photographs, drawings, etc.) available on the Internet, you will need a good quality monitor that supports at least 256 colors. Monitors that support thousands and millions of colors are also available. Be aware that high-end, large screen monitors may require the addition of special parts called video cards installed into your computer.

Peripherals

Peripherals are things that you add to your computer, such as CD-ROMs, printers, scanners, modems, video input cards, digital cameras, etc., that will enhance what your computer will do. When shopping for peripherals, study the job that you want to do and the software you need to do it.

1. What quality are you expecting?
2. What will you need to add to your computer for the peripheral to work?
3. Does the peripheral require any software?

CONNECTING TO THE INTERNET *(cont.)*

STEPS TO CONNECTING TO THE INTERNET THROUGH A COMMERCIAL ONLINE SERVICE

For this example we will use America Online. Other COSs like Compuserve and Prodigy use much the same procedure. This assumes that you have followed the instructions and installed the software on your hard drive.

1. Launch the program as you would any other program.

2. You will be greeted by a screen much like this one.

3. Type in your password in the area provided. You should have selected a password when you installed and set up the program.

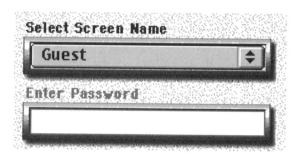

CONNECTING TO THE INTERNET *(cont.)*

4. Click Connect or Sign On.

5. Once you are connected you will see a menu for the service. This is NOT the Internet. You are now on the commercial service only—like connecting to a big computer somewhere out there in cyberspace. There are several things you can do here, but the amount of information and services, although staggering, pales in comparison to what awaits you on the Internet.

6. On AOL, like most COS's, getting to the Internet is as easy as clicking a button that says Internet Connection.

You are now officially a surfer!

CONNECTING TO THE INTERNET *(cont.)*

STEPS TO CONNECTING TO THE INTERNET THROUGH AN INTERNET SERVICE PROVIDER

Connecting to the Internet through an ISP is much like connecting through a COS. These steps assume that you have already installed the software and followed the directions given to set up your account. All ISPs are a little different in the way that they handle this, so follow directions closely.

1. Launch your connection program, probably a PPP or SLIP program, and click connect.

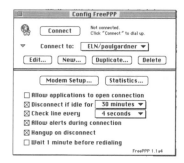

2. You may have to put in the password that you were provided when you set up your account.

3. You are then given some indication that the connection was successful.

4. If successfully connected, launch your browsing program and you are online.

Look out world, you are connected!

ELECTRONIC MAIL

Electronic Mail or e-mail is the easiest and most common use of the Internet. Once you have an e-mail address, you will be able to send and receive correspondence with others on the Internet much like you do with regular postal mail. The difference between e-mail and postal mail (commonly called snail mail by Internauts) is that it is delivered almost immediately. In addition, you can "enclose" or "attach" other electronic materials like documents, files, or programs. These will be taken, along with the message, to the recipient of your mail.

When you gain Internet access through an Internet Service Provider or a Commercial Network Service, you are normally given an e-mail address automatically (e.g., "paulgardner@techknowledgey.com"). These addresses are unique so that computer routers can locate the recipient and deliver the mail. Making mistakes in the spelling, spacing, punctuation, or case may result in the mail being returned to you undelivered.

THE ANATOMY OF AN E-MAIL ADDRESS

E-mail addresses have three distinctive parts as shown in the diagram below:

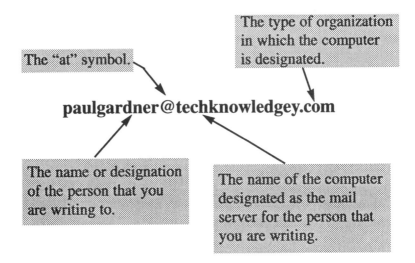

The "at" symbol.

The type of organization in which the computer is designated.

paulgardner@techknowledgey.com

The name or designation of the person that you are writing to.

The name of the computer designated as the mail server for the person that you are writing.

ELECTRONIC MAIL *(cont.)*

The suffix after the decimal point will tell you what type of service is providing the e-mail account. A few of the suffixes include:

Suffix	Type of Provider
.edu	educational
.com	commercial or business
.org	non-profit organization
.gov	government
.mil	military
.net	networking provider

Some of the more popular e-mail providers addressing styles are listed below. "User" refers to the User's identification or registered name. It is generally accepted that e-mail addresses are in all lower case. Several commercial services allow their users to use uppercase letters, however, if you are not sure about the case, always use lower. The e-mails will be delivered in this way.

Provider	Addressing
America Online	user@aol.com
Compuserve	user.user@compuserve.com
Prodigy	user@prodigy.com
MicroSoft Network	user@msn.com

WRITING E-MAIL

Writing a basic e-mail message is simple. Although each e-mail program has different bells and whistles, they are all similar in the way that they send basic messages. For the following example, *Claris Emailer* will be used to demonstrate how to send a basic e-mail message.

You must first launch your e-mail program. This can be done prior to connecting to the Internet or while online. (Refer to your manual for steps to launch your e-mail program.) Most will come up with several directories from which to choose.

24

ELECTRONIC MAIL *(cont.)*

In order to send e-mail you will want to choose new mail. This is usually in a menu at the top of the screen or a separate button.

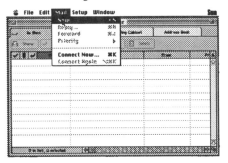

Once you have new mail, there are two items that are necessary to fill in: the recipient area and the message area. Once the e-mail has been completed, it is either saved for later delivery or sent immediately, depending on whether or not you are connected at the time.

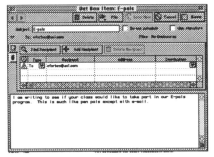

Other items that can be filled in include the folowing:

- **Subject:** (Optional but recommended) Should describe the message.
- **Cc:** (Optional) E-mail addresses of people who you want to send a carbon copy of the message to.
- **Bcc:** (Optional) E-mail addresses of people who you want to send a blind carbon copy to. The recipients will not see these people's names in the message.
- **Reply to:** (Optional) Address that you want replies to be sent to if different than the originator's.
- **Date:** (Required and automatic) Date and time that the message was sent.
- **Expires:** (Optional) Date that the message will expire and not be sent.

ELECTRONIC MAIL *(cont.)*

SENDING ATTACHMENTS

Let's say that you have a friend who you want to send a word processing document or neat piece of free software to. Most programs allow you to "attach" or "enclose" these electronic files to your e-mail. You simply click the attachment or enclosure button (or select attachment or enclosure) from a menu, then navigate to where the file is that you want to enclose. This is done differently depending on the type of computer you have. With Windows based computers the file will be located in the directory that you saved it in, whereas Macintosh computers save documents in folders. Consult your manual as to the the way your computer system locates files.

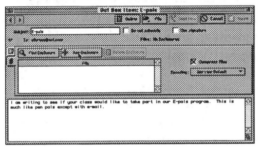

ORGANIZING YOUR E-MAIL

All e-mail programs include an address book feature. This feature allows you to keep track of your e-mail adresses by sorting them with the owners real name. You can even organize the addresses in special groups.

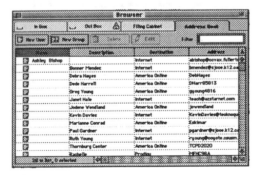

E-mail Advice: Put all the e-mail addresses of teachers into a group called Teachers. When you need materials, ideas, or advice, just send an e-mail making the request addressed to the whole group. The e-mail is sent to all of the people in your list at the same time.

ELECTRONIC MAIL *(cont.)*

RECEIVING MAIL

Receiving mail addressed to you is as easy as a click of the mouse. Your commercial Internet service provider has what is called a mail server. This is a computer that holds your mail until you sign on or "come to get it." To get your mail you must first connect to your Internet service. (See pages 20–22.) Once connected to the service you start your e-mail software and click on or find in a menu "Get Mail."

Note: Some e-mail programs automatically get mail when they are started.

Each e-mail software notifies you a little differently when you have mail. Some emit a tone or recorded voice, "You have mail!" While others simply flash an icon or show an animation of a letter going into a mail box.

The e-mail will be displayed in a list and organized by date sent, author, or subject.

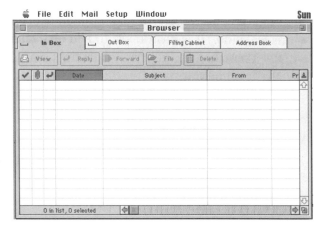

REPLYING AND FORWARDING MAIL

Once mail has been received you can reply to the sender simply by clicking or choosing Reply. The reply is automatically addressed and the subject line is filled in with Re: Subject. Most e-mail programs can be set to quote the original note. Quoted lines will be preceded by the > sign.

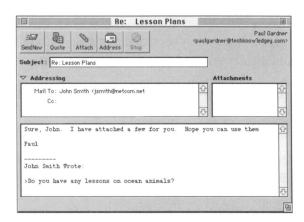

ELECTRONIC MAIL *(cont.)*

Forwarding an e-mail to a person is even easier. Clicking or choosing the Forward command will attach the original message to a new e-mail. Just address it to the person you want to forward the e-mail to, add a note of your own, and click or choose send.

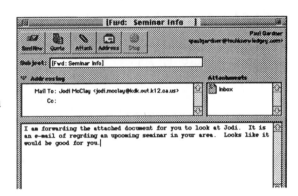

EMOTICONS

Although it is customary to make e-mail short and concise, it is not without its whimsical side. It is customary to add characters that express emotions to e-mail. These are normal type characters that look like faces on their sides. A few are listed below.

: - 0	Expresses shock or bewilderment
: -)	Expresses happiness
: - (	Expresses unhappiness
; -)	Indicates an inside joke or sarcasm

WHAT CAN I DO WITH E-MAIL

Aside from the obvious use of e-mail to communicate with friends and colleagues, e-mail in the classroom can be used for several educational purposes. Some of those include the following:

E-pals: Become cyberspace pen pals with other students around the world. You not only correspond, but cooperate on research and share projects.

Electronic Expeditions: Students can ask questions and/or read reports on a variety of topics, from a wagon train going west, to the space shuttle, to the Iditorad, to a South American bike expedition to name a few.

Request Information: There are many resources in which parents, students, and teachers can request information for research they are conducting.

Collaboration: Collaborate with other classes or teachers from around the world on projects or lessons.

MAILING LISTS

The advent of e-mail has spawned an exchange of ideas via this tool called mailing lists or Listservs. At last estimate there were thousands of these lists, each on a specific topic. To illustrate how this works let's look at an education example.

If you were interested in sharing ideas with other educators you might join a Listserv like EDNet. This list boasts over 4,000 members from around the world. Once a member, you could send e-mail messages to the entire group by addressing it to the list. Ask a question, request ideas, or answer other's requests. You become a member of a group of professionals that help each other. There are two different types of listservs: moderated and unmoderated. In a moderated list, an administrator views all the mail and only forwards the good ones to the list members. Many frequently asked questions or FAQs are not forwarded to save list users valuable time. Mail including FAQs are referred to a FAQs file. Other mail which has no value is simply destroyed before it reaches the list members. You can imagine with member lists sometimes in the thousands, moderated lists can cut down on the sheer amount of mail that the members get. Administrators will often correct users by sending mail back to originators who don't follow the rules of the list. Members can also be removed from the list for not obeying the rules.

Unmoderated lists are in comparison as valuable, but can waste members' time. Unmoderated lists tend to be self-governing. Members many times will correct other users' conduct on the list.

SUBSCRIBING TO A MAILING LIST

Once you have found a mailing list to which you would like to become a member, follow the steps below to join.

1. Create an e-mail message and address it to the mailing list. (See page 30.)
2. Usually you will need to leave the subject line blank.
3. Check the FAQs for the list of specifics.
4. In the body of the mail, type subscribe <listserv> <Your Name> (e.g., subscribe IECC Pauline Boyd).

MAILING LISTS *(cont.)*

Most of the lists are automated, meaning you will be added automatically by the computer that the list resides on. So it is important that you type the subscriptions completely and accurately. You will be notified when you are added to a new list.

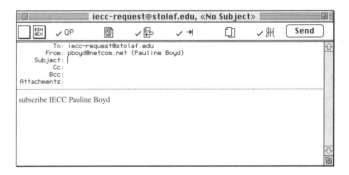

UNSUBSCRIBING TO A MAILING LIST

It is conceivable that you could receive 100s of e-mails a day from list members. This is usually not the case however, but an active list could have several posts a day. There will come a time that you will need a break from the list. Especially if you are going to be unable to access you mail for a few days. In fact, many people subscribe and unsubscribe to lists when they have to get a question answered. This is acceptable, however, it is good to give what you receive. If you can, answer a few e-mails or join in on a discussion. The list is only as helpful as its members.

To unsubscribe, repeat the directions for subscribing above and substitute the word unsubscribe. You will again get an automated confirmation that you have unsubscribed.

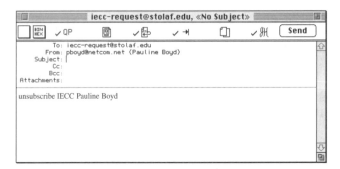

MAILING LISTS *(cont.)*

SOME EDUCATIONAL MAILING LISTS

BILINGUE-L
Developmental bilingual elementary education list
Address: listserv@Reynolds.k12.or.us.

CHILDRENS-VOICE
Publishes writing from children ages 5-14
Address: listproc@scholnet.carleton.ca.

COSNDISC
Consortium for School Networking
Address: listproc@yukon.cren.org

ECENET-L
Early childhood education list
Address: listserv@uiucvmd.bitnet.

EDINFO-L
Contains information related to educational issues
Address: edinfo-l@iubvm.ucs.indiana.edu

EDTECH
Information on educational technology
Address: listserv@msu.edu

ELEMUG
Elementary School Users' Group
Address: listserv@uicvm.uic.edu.

GRANTS-L
NSF grants information list
Address: listserv@onondaga.bitnet.

IECC
Intercultural E-Mail Classroom Connections
Address: iecc-request@stolaf.edu

K12-AUP
Acceptable Use Policies discussion
Address: k12-aup-request@merit.edu

MAILING LISTS *(cont.)*

SOME EDUCATIONAL MAILING LISTS *(cont.)*

KIDLINK
Activity projects for kids
Address: listserv@vm1.nodak.edu.

KIDOPEDIA
About creation of the kidopedia sites around the world and related issues
Address:listserv@sjuvm.stjohns.edu

KIDSPHERE
International kid's dialog
Address: kidsphere-request@vms.cis.pitt.edu

MATHSED-L
Discussion group on Mathematics in Education
Address: listserv@deakin.edu.au.

MEDIA-L
Focuses on the role of the media in education
Address: listserv@bingvmb.cc.binghamton.edu

MMEDIA-L
Discussions of multimedia in education
Address: listserv@vmtecmex.bitnet

MIDDLE-L
Discussion of middle school-aged children
Address: listserv@vmd.cso.uiuc.edu.

MUSIC-ED
Music education discussion
Address: listserv@artsedge.kennedy-center.org.

NARST-L
Focuses on teaching science; sponsored by the National Association for Research in Science Teaching
Address: listserv@uwf.bitnet

TAG-L
A Talented and Gifted List
Address: Listserv@ndsuvm1.nodak.edu

UAARTED
Art education discussion
Address: listserv@arizvm1.bitnet.

FILE TRANSFER PROTOCOL

File Transfer Protocol or FTP is what is used to send and receive files. "And what, pray tell, do you mean by files?" you may be asking at this point. Anything that can be stored on a computer can be sent over the Internet. Documents, pictures, movies, sounds, software programs, etc. can all be sent using FTP. There are millions of programs deemed shareware and freeware that are out there on someone's computer waiting to be copied and transferred to your computer. Choose from millions of lesson plans, digital pictures for reports, video clips for presentations, and books.

RECEIVING FILES

In order to receive or download files using FTP, you will need the following:

- the URL (address) of the FTP site
- the name of the directory where the file is located
- the name of the file

At one time finding this information was tricky, but since the invention of graphical interfaces like *Netscape* and *Internet Explorer* and the several search mechanisms that are available on the World Wide Web, finding these files is much easier. (See Search for WWW, Usenet Newsgroups, and Gopher Sites, page 57.)

Once you have located the required information for downloading (transferring a file from another computer to yours) a particular file, you will need to use a piece of FTP software to retrieve it. Once again, graphical Internet browser software usually is all you need to carry out the FTP functions that you need to receive files. For this demonstration we will use *Netscape Navigator* to transfer a shareware program called *GradeKeeper*. Try downloading this file, it is a great grade managment program and you can use it free for 30 days.

1. Log-on to your Internet Service Provider or Commercial Online Service. (See Connecting, pages 20–22.)

2. Once you have connected, start your browser and click the Open button or choose Open from the menu bar.

FILE TRANSFER PROTOCOL *(cont.)*

3. Type in the URL of the site in which the file is located and click Open File.

4. Find the directory in which the file is located and click it to open.

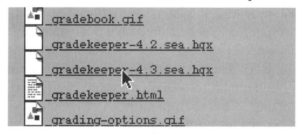

5. Find the file that you wish to download and click it. A copy of the file will download to your computer.

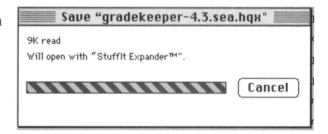

Files that are downloaded from the Internet are normally compressed to save space on servers and time downloading. Macintosh files are normally stuffed with a program called StuffIt. Windows programs are normally zipped with a program called PK Zip or WinZip. Most ISPs provide this software at the time you sign up for their service and are set up to automatically decompress files after download. If you do not have this software installed, you can obtain them at www.shareware.com.

PLACING A FILE

Placing a file or uploading onto another computer is not any more difficult than retrieving, however, most computers are protected from this being done. When retrieving a file from a server (i.e., a computer that is designated to give files) you will normally be using an anonymous FTP site. This means there are no particular security measures for accessing the files. Uploading, on the other hand, is normally done on a secured FTP site. These sites, for obvious reasons, require a password to place files there. If you have an occasion to upload files to a site (like when establishing your own Web page), you will probably be directed as to the procedure needed to do this from the server's administrator. For this reason we will not cover it here.

GOPHER

Before the digital spider began to spin what is the World Wide Web, there was that wily rodent of the Internet: the Gopher. Although the Web is the information gathering tool of choice, Gopher continues to be an easy, efficient tool to use when searching for text and downloading pictures.

Gopher is a menu based information system that allows for broad searches of information. If your Internet connection is the easy to use graphical, point and click type, Gopher sites are easy to navigate through. They are also much faster than most Web pages due to their lack of graphics. Graphics take much longer to download than text. You simply choose the menu that matches the subject you are interested in, point the mouse at it, then click. Each menu narrows until you reach the information that you are looking for. For example, if you are looking for lesson plans to go with a unit you are teaching on Space your search may look like the following:

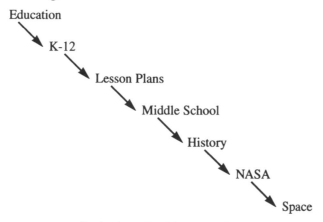

Once you arrive you may find a hundred lesson plans dealing with Space.

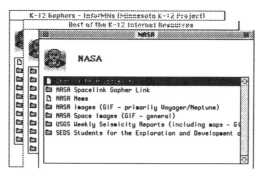

GOPHER *(cont.)*

GETTING INFORMATION WITH GOPHER

Using an Internet browsing program like *Netscape* makes getting and retrieving information from a Gopher site very easy. First, establish your connection with your ISP or COS and launch your browsing program. (See Connecting, pages 20–22.)

If you know the URL (address) of the Gopher server use the Open command to type in the URL (address). We will be using the Ask Eric Gopher to

demonstrate. Let's pretend that we are looking for a math lesson plan for teaching basic math facts.

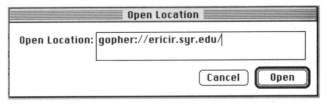

Once at the Gopher site you will notice the menu has two different types of icons. Folder icons which represent sub-menus and document icons which represent documents that can be reviewed. In this case we will open the sub-menu for lesson plans.

You can continue to move down through sub menus until you find what you are looking for. Each folder will open by clicking on it. It is possible for you to find folders within folders. If you continue to break down these subject folders, eventually all that will be left are documents.

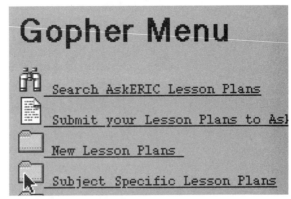

Until you finally arrive at the subject of your search. This window shows a list of lesson plans. In order to view a lesson plan, just click the name or document icon that is associated with the one that you want to view.

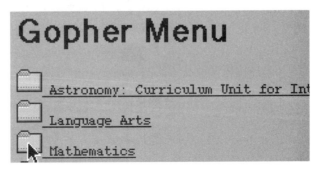

GOPHER *(cont.)*

Note: This window shows only a few of the over 100 lesson plans that are available in this sub menu. To see more, you would have to scroll through the list, something we have not learned how to do yet.

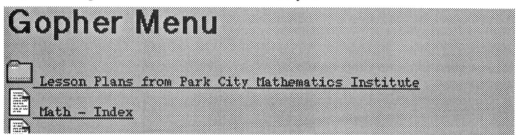

Below is the top portion of a lesson plan.

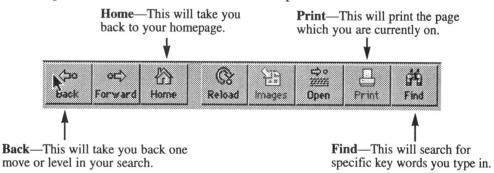

Note: The URL for this site at the top of your browser is now a culmination of the menus and sub menus in which you have traveled.

gopher://ericir.syr.edu:70/00/Lesson/Subject/Math/cecmath.02

There are several things you can do at this point. In *Netscape*, *Internet Explorer*, *AOL Web Crawler*, as well as other web browsers, you are given a set of buttons that have special functions that work well in Gopher.

Home—This will take you back to your homepage.

Print—This will print the page which you are currently on.

Back—This will take you back one move or level in your search.

Find—This will search for specific key words you type in.

GOPHER *(cont.)*

FINDING GOPHER SERVERS

Finding Gophers can be easy in your yard. Just look for the tell-tale mound of dirt. However, on the Internet, you have to ask around. One of the best places to ask is the Great Mother Gopher. No, this isn't some huge rodent sitting around waiting to tell you where her offspring are, but close. Gopher was developed as a project by students and staff at the University of Minnesota. The mascot of UM is, you guessed it, the Golden Gopher.

GOPHER SEARCHES

There are many other Gopher searching tools that can help you find the information you are looking for. These tools search computers all over the world looking for information that you request. For example, if you wanted to see information about K-12 education, you would simply enter this information into the search tool by typing the keywords "K-12 education" into the search box. It is suggested that, because of ease of use, the novice Internet explorer should make every attempt to use a web browsing program like *Netscape* or *IE*, as these programs allow them to take full advantage of most of these search tools in a graphic, point and click, environment.

Some of the search tools that are associated with Gopher are listed below.

Veronica: A search tool that allows the user to input a keyword to search the entire Internet.

Jughead: Like Veronica, Jughead searches for information using a keyword but on a single Gopher site or area of the Internet.

Archie: Archie is much more specific. You will have to know at least part of a filename that you are looking for.

WAIS (Wide Area Information Search): WAIS is used for very specific searches. In WAIS the user enters the specific information needed, such as "recent research dealing with caught in the middle." WAIS then searches looking for information dealing with this subject.

You can usually find these tools at the Gopher sites that you visit on your travels through Gopherspace.

GOPHER *(cont.)*

GREAT GOPHERS

The following is a list of great education Gopher sites.

Name: Ties Best With K–12 Gopher

Description: This Gopher has lists of Gopher servers, World Wide Web sites, Telnet sites, FTP sites, Mailing Lists (listservs), Library Catalogs, Classroom Activities and Projects, Publications, Notices, News Flashes, and Other Short-Term Information, FYI (FAQs, training aids, and other resources).

URL: gopher://informns.k12.mn.us:70/11/best-k12

Name: Lesson Plans on the Internet

Description: Find these education jewels at this Gopher: TIES's Best of the K-12 Internet Resources, Goldmine of Educational, Mailing List Archives, Assorted Lesson Plans, Teacher Resources for Educational Projects, K-12 Educational Resources from CoSN, Disability Information, KIDLINK Gopher, NASA'S K-12 Gopher, and Research for Better Schools.

URL: gopher://bvsd.k12.co.us:70/11/Educational_Resources

USENET NEWSGROUPS

Usenet groups are much like listservs in the fact that they are dialogs divided into specific subjects. The difference, however, is that usenet groups are more like a virtual bulletin board. Let's say that you are in the teachers' lounge and you place a note asking for lesson plans on that inevitable corkboard that one finds in this oasis of sanity. You come back to the board later in the afternoon and find ten different lesson plans pinned to the board under your note. This is a simplified usenet group. In usenet, you can read original postings in topic areas of interest, then read responses to those postings. A big difference from listservs is that you do not have to join a usenet group. You can read any posting in any group that you want.

There are more than 15,000 usenet message boards (groups) and the number grows every day with subjects ranging from the mundane to the intellectual, the most popular newsgroup categories include the following: computers, business, biology, recreation, science, social issues, miscellaneous, alternative discussions, and, of course, K–12 education. There are more than 400 usenets just devoted to education. Some of these groups are visited by hundreds of people every day while others have few frequenters. You can even start your own newsgroup.

Most of these groups are unmoderated, meaning you can post directly to the group. Moderated newsgroups are censored by a moderator who posts only those messages he/she thinks are of interest to the group. Once the message is posted, anyone can respond.

Each newsgroup has a name that is a series of words and abbreviations separated by decimal points or dots as they have come to be known in Internet-ese. Let's dissect a newsgroup name.

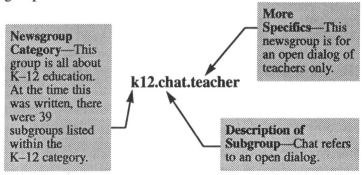

Newsgroup Category—This group is all about K–12 education. At the time this was written, there were 39 subgroups listed within the K–12 category.

More Specifics—This newsgroup is for an open dialog of teachers only.

k12.chat.teacher

Description of Subgroup—Chat refers to an open dialog.

USENET NEWSGROUPS *(cont.)*

SUBSCRIBING TO NEWSGROUPS

"I thought you said that you didn't have to join a newsgroup!" is probably what you're thinking. You are right. Subscribing is really not a good word, but it is the one that is used. Subscribing to newsgroups is really only choosing the ones that you want to view and take part in. With over 15,000 newsgroups, there is no way that you would want to look at all of them. In fact, you will find some useless and others downright offensive. So subscribing is just choosing to view certain newsgroups and eliminating the others.

The first thing that you will need in order to choose, read, and post newsgroups is a newsreader software program. Today's graphical browsers handle this job well. We will again use *Netscape* and an Internet service provider's PPP connection to demonstrate how you view a usenet newsgroup. Remember, that different software is going to arrange things a little differently, but they all carry out essentially the same functions.

1. First you must connect to your ISP or COS and launch your newsgroup software. (See Connecting, pages 20–22.)

2. Now select View All Newsgroups. It may take a few minutes for your computer to download the entire list.

Note: This may not be ALL the newsgroups that are available. That will depend on your ISP or COS. These companies very seldom provide ALL the newsgroups. If you find out about a newsgroup that is not available through your service, e-mail them and ask that it be added. This can take anywhere from a few hours to a few days to be completed.

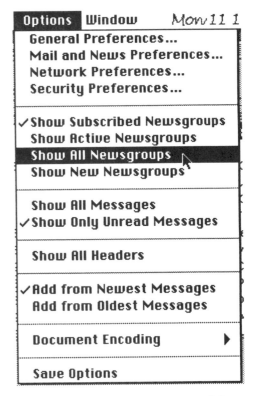

USENET NEWSGROUPS *(cont.)*

3. Next, look at the list and choose the groups that you would like to subscribe to. In *Netscape* it is done by simply clicking a checkmark in the subscribe column. Other software may have you do this differently.

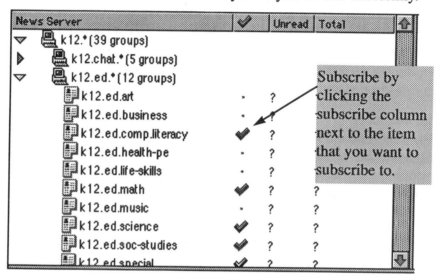

4. Once you have subscribed to all the newsgroups that are of interest to you select Show Subscribed List to see your newsgroups.

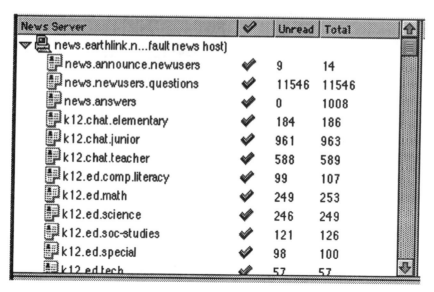

USENET NEWSGROUPS *(cont.)*

READING MESSAGES

Reading messages is just a snap. All you have to do is choose the Newsgroup that you wish to view and a list of those postings will appear.

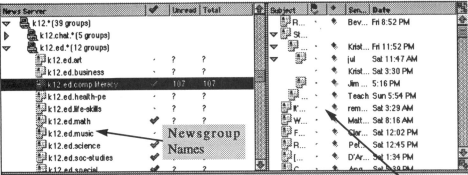

Click a posting and the message will appear.

TYPICAL POSTING

Postings include the following information:

Subject: Make sure that this is short and to the point. If a message is in reference to an original then it will begin with Re:

Date: The date and time that the post was made. This is inputted automatically.

From: The e-mail address of the person who posted the message.

Newsgroups: The newsgroups in which the message was posted. Be careful with multiple postings. You should make sure that the message will be appropriate for the newsgroup in which it is posted.

Body: The message itself. Describe your need or comment as briefly as you can.

The following is a typical posting that you might find at a newsgroup.

> Subject: Ideas for Inventions
> Date: Sun, 06 Sept 96 15:30:59
> From: psi@netx.net
> Newsgroups: k12.chat.teacher.k12.ed.math.k12.ed.science
>
> Hello,
> My 4th grader has a school project to invent something. I have searched the Net, but found nothing. Any ideas or pointers to sources welcome.

USENET NEWSGROUPS *(cont.)*

POSTING MESSAGES

Before posting a message to a usenet newsgroup, spend a few days reading the existing posts. This is called lurking. Also read the FAQs (frequently asked questions), these are usually the first postings in a newsgroup. Doing these things will help you to get familiar with the protocol for newsgroups and reduce your chance of getting "flamed" (sent a note that is derogatory in nature). Here are some of your options when posting messages.

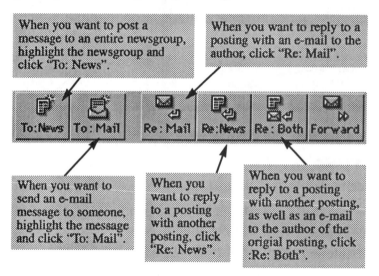

POPULAR EDUCATIONAL USENET NEWSGROUPS

The following is a list of usenet groups that are popular with K–12 educators.

Learning for the disabled
alt.education.disabled

Children in a split family
alt.child-support

Discussions about raising teenagers
alt.parents-teens

Chat for elementary students
k12.chat.elementary

USENET NEWSGROUPS *(cont.)*

Chat for middle school students
k12.chat.junior

Chat for among teachers
k12.chat.teacher

Art curriculum
k12.ed.art

Teaching computer literacy
k12.ed.comp.literacy

Health and physical education curriculum
k12.ed.health-pe

Home economics and career education
k12.ed.life-skills

Mathematics curriculum
k12.ed.math

Music and performing arts curriculum
k12.ed.music

Science curriculum
k12.ed.science

Social studies and history curriculum
k12.ed.soc-studies

Information for teachers of students with special needs
k12.ed.special

Education for talented and gifted students
k12.ed.tag

Language arts curriculum
k12.lang.art

Bilingual German/English practice with native speakers
k12.lang.deutsch-eng

Bilingual Spanish/English practice with native speakers
k12.lang.esp-eng

THE WORLD WIDE WEB

The World Wide Web, which is also known as WWW or the Web, is the fastest growing segment of the Internet. The reason for the Web's overwhelming success is its ease of navigation and its media rich environment. Early Internet explorers had to input long strings of text that directed them to their destination. Once there they were hampered by continually typing commands to retrieve information. This is not the case with the WWW.

You cannot flip to a page in a magazine or turn to a channel on television these days without receiving an invitation by businesses, government, educational institutions, etc. to visit them on the World Wide Web. Since 1992, this Internet phenomenon has grown somewhere in the neighborhood of 300,000% and although it is slowing somewhat, it continues to grow at an awesome rate. But what is it?

WHAT IS THE WORLD WIDE WEB?

Simply put, the Web is a series of interconnected documents and pages. We will use the analogy of a library to help explain this concept. A book in this library might have connections or links to several other books or pieces of media. For example, if you were looking at a book on the Seven Wonders of the World and were reading about the Great Pyramids, you might find a reference to another book about the pyramids. So you pick up the other book and read. You then find a reference in that book about a photograph on microfilm. So you go and view the microfilm and print a copy of the picture, but on the microfilm there is a reference to a movie about the Pyramid at Giza. You make the trip across the library to the media center where you view the movie. This movie might even have a reference back to the original book you were reading or to some other material.

Using the World Wide Web is like using a super library, if you will. You can move from site to site, from document to document, from page to film clip, from sound clip to document, millions of different connections to millions of different computers all over the world—thus a world wide web of connections.

THE WORLD WIDE WEB *(cont.)*

CONNECTING TO THE WEB

In order to access the Web, you must have a Web browsing program. The most popular browsing programs are *Netscape* and *Mosaic*. However, if you are connected to a commercial service provider like America Online or Compuserve, they usually have their own web browser.

The browsing software you use will dictate which tools are available to you. Some browsing programs will allow you to download sounds and motion pictures and others will not. Web browsers have also integrated all the older Internet navigation tools like e-mail (electronic mail), FTP (file transfer protocol), TELNET, as well as other information search tools into one software package. This has made using the Internet simple for even novice users.

Connecting to the World Wide Web is no different than connecting to any other part of the Internet using a browsing program like *Netscape*. Getting to and retrieving information from a Web site is very simple. First establish your connection with your ISP or COS and launch your browsing program. (See Connecting, pages 20–22.)

WEB PAGES AND WEB SITES

The WWW is based on millions of interconnected electronic pages called Web pages. When you connect to the Web the first thing that you will see is something called your homepage. Let's say that you entered a library and you were looking for information on animals for student reports. You would first see the sign outside and maybe some directory information to guide you to the right part of the library. In Web terms, this would be your home page. A homepage is your starting point for your information search. It is the page that your browser automatically goes to when you start it. Most Web browsing programs ship with the publisher's page or your ISP or COS's page as the home page. This can be changed by the user. You can even write your own page. See an example of a school homepage on page 55.

THE WORLD WIDE WEB *(cont.)*

WEB BASICS

Moving around on the Web is very easy. If you know how to point and click a mouse, you have the basic skills to move through the Web and view its resources.

Hypertext is the first vehicle that you will use. Those areas of text that are a different color than the rest are "hyper." If you place your mouse's cursor over this colored text, you will notice that the arrow becomes a hand with a finger pointing. Many times hypertext is also underlined, this means that if you click the text something will happen. Most of the time you will jump to another web page or another area of the page but these hypertext links, as they are called, can do much more. You can download images, sounds, or even movies. Reading the text itself will give you an idea of what the text does.

Subject Access

Arts and Literature
Business Sources & Grants
Education Resources
Entertainment & Travel
Health, P.E., & Fitness
History & Social Studies
Hobbies
Holidays
Humor
Kidstuff

Mathematics
News Sources & Magazines
Organizations & Government
Reference Sources
Science & Technology
Shopping
Sports
Vocational Education
Weather
World Cultures & Regions

Hypermedia are pictures that do the same thing as hypertext. Many are in the form of buttons or icons. New web browsers even allow for animated hypermedia graphics. Most hypermedia graphics are outlined in a color, which is usually blue. However, this is not always the case. Remember if your cursor turns into a finger when it passes over a graphic, it is probably "hyper."

THE WORLD WIDE WEB *(cont.)*

Imagemaps work like hypermedia except clicking different parts of the picture area will take you to different places. Normally the picture indicates in some way where you will be transported when you click it.

Automatic (Inline) Graphics are those pictures that you see automatically when you arrive at a web page. Most web browsers give you the option to view web pages without these graphics. This will speed up the loading of the page, but it is not very pretty.

Requested Graphics only appear after you ask to see them by clicking a link. After clicking the link, a blank page appears to display the image. Large pictures can take a long time to download and view. Sometimes web writers provide you with a thumbnail (i.e., a tiny form of the picture), so you can decide if you really want the picture before downloading it.

NAVIGATING THE WEB

Getting around on the web is not really all that difficult. It is like using the library. If you were looking for information in a library, you would either browse through the aisles looking for the right section (Browsing or Surfing), go to a librarian and ask for help (Directories), or search through a card catalog to locate a specific book or group of books (Search Engines). The Web offers you the same types of options.

THE WORLD WIDE WEB *(cont.)*

BROWSING OR SURFING THE WEB

Every Web page has a uniform resource locator or URL. This is a techy's way of saying address. There are several ways to get to homepages that contain information you want to see. One way is to simply enter the URL of a homepage into the location line of the Web browser and press Return or Enter. These URLs are not hard to find. All you have to do is peruse magazines or watch television these days to find dozens of them. The URL to the Whitehouse, one of the most visited homepages on the Web, is http://www.whitehouse.gov.

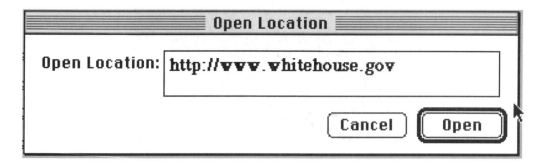

From existing pages you can continue to try different links to search out information. This process is very time consuming, though.

SEARCH ENGINES

One of the best ways to find information on the Web or any other Internet resource, is to use a search engine, the card catalog of the Internet. There are several commercial companies providing search engines free of charge to the public. Free, you say? Yes, as free as television and radio. You will notice that when you use these tools you are bombarded with advertising. The other thing that you will notice is that the advertising is pinpointed to whatever you are requesting in the search. For example, if you are looking for information about lesson plans, you might see an advertisement for an educational software program with your results. Usually the ads are hypermedia that link you to the advertiser's Web site. This is a free market economy at work. Remember, nothing is completely free.

THE WORLD WIDE WEB *(cont.)*

To use a search engine, first go to that engine's page. A list of good search engines are listed on page 57. In most cases you will be greeted with a form that allows you to input keywords that might be in the description of the site that you are looking for. We will use Yahoo's

search engine to try to find links to Children's literature resources. You can narrow the search to just education if you do not want commercial sites to show in your search.

Click the search button and Yahoo will give you a list of sites on children's literature. Yahoo found 98 sites that included children's literature in their description. A few are listed to the right.

Note: To narrow searches, read Search Help provided at the search engines' site.

UNIFORM RESOURCE LOCATOR

Every resource has a uniform resource locator or URL. This is a techy's way of saying address. Let's look at what

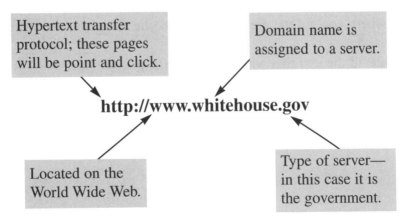

Hypertext transfer protocol; these pages will be point and click.

Domain name is assigned to a server.

http://www.whitehouse.gov

Located on the World Wide Web.

Type of server— in this case it is the government.

THE WORLD WIDE WEB *(cont.)*

MAKING YOUR OWN HOMEPAGE

One of the most fantastic things about the World Wide Web is that it is a place where you as an individual can have a presence. In fact, many people are amazed at how easy it is to author and maintain your own homepage on the Web. Classrooms, schools, districts, and parent groups do it all the time. This is a super class project and can be divided into cooperative groups.

STEPS TO PLANNING A HOMEPAGE

1. Make decisions of what you want the world to see? There are several examples of classroom web pages at Web66 (http://web66.coled.umn.edu/) and Yahoo's Education K-12 (http:www.yahoo.com/Education/K_12).

   Some ideas are as follows:
   - About the teacher
   - About the class
   - Activities done during the year
   - Interactive projects
   - Home-school communication
   - Links to sites that enhance your curriculum

2. After viewing examples, design your Web page on a piece of paper. You can have a design contest in class.
   - Decide on complementary colors for the page's background, lines, icons, bullets, and other dots.
   - Look at sites where free web art is available. See page 58 for ideas about bullets, lines, icons, and other graphics. Remember to keep track of where you got the graphics from, so you can give the artist credit on your page.
   - Write all the text that will be used on the page using a word processor. This way you can easily edit and spell check the document. Then just copy and paste the text into your web editor.
   - Have any photographs digitally developed or scan existing pictures. Digital cameras also work well.

THE WORLD WIDE WEB *(cont.)*

- Organize all your resources into a single file and label all with names that you will remember. Make sure that file extensions like .jpeg, .gif, and .text are present on all files.
- All graphic files will have to be converted to JPEG or GIF files. This can be done in most paint or draw programs, as well as Web creation tools. (See page 58.)

3. Put your page together using the resources you have collected.

- Spend some time learning html or working with your Web creation tool. (See page 58 for a list of easy to use tools.) If you don't want to have to learn how to make Web pages, check with your ISP or your parents to see if either one would be willing to help.

- Insert graphics and text

- Program the links

- Mount the page on a server. Several ISPs and COSs provide their users with web space. Check with yours or your school's providers to see if they will provide space. Web66—(http://web66.coled.umn.edu) provides information on how to get your page on the web.

- Test your Web site.

4. Announce your Web page to the world.

- Have a Web page unveiling party.

- Send notes home.

- Call the local newspaper.

- Register it with several search engines. (See page 57.)

5. Start all over with revisions. Web pages are a work in progress.

THE WORLD WIDE WEB *(cont.)*

SAMPLE PERSONAL HOMEPAGE

Teacher Resources|Kids' Places|Keypals|Video-Conference|Freebies|Search| Sign My Guestbook

---

Hello and welcome to my home on the web. I teach Title 1 Reading/Language Arts to first and second graders at ▨▨▨▨▨ in Lewisburg, Tennessee. I have internet access (ISDN) in my classroom and video-conference capability. These pages contain links that I have found useful. Stay a while and look around a bit or just follow the links and check out all the teacher resources and school stuff. This page is updated regularly so check back often to see what's new.

Check out your weather forecast at **NETCAST** or you can see what the weather is like here in **Lewisburg, Tennessee.**

Just For Fun

Find today's TV Listings or see the latest Movie Reviews.

Cool School Sites

- Walpole Elementary School HomePage
- International School of Stavanger, The City of Stavanger
- ▨▨ Maryland Virtual High School (Check out the projects.)
- Park School, African American Heroes
- Fremont High - Astronomy Home Page

THE WORLD WIDE WEB *(cont.)*

SAMPLE SCHOOL HOMEPAGE

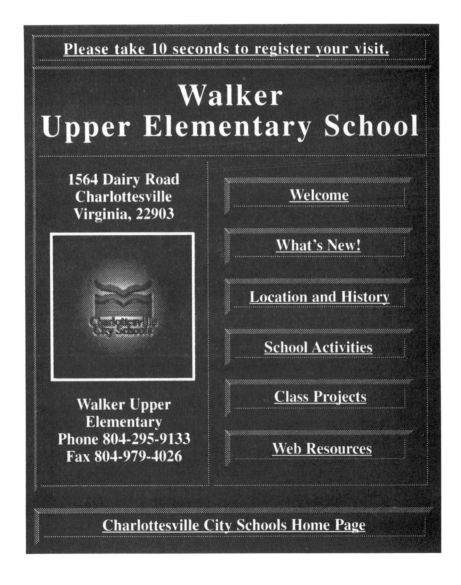

Please take 10 seconds to register your visit.

Walker Upper Elementary School

1564 Dairy Road
Charlottesville
Virginia, 22903

Walker Upper
Elementary
Phone 804-295-9133
Fax 804-979-4026

Welcome

What's New!

Location and History

School Activities

Class Projects

Web Resources

Charlottesville City Schools Home Page

THE WORLD WIDE WEB *(cont.)*

SAMPLE CLASS HOMEPAGE

| Room 10 |
| Room 10 |
| Room 10 |
| Room 10 |
| Room 10 |
| Room 10 |
| Room 10 |
| Room 10 |
| Room 10 |
| Room 10 |
| Room 10 |
| Room 10 |

Le Grand Elementary School
Fifth Grade

Welcome to our classroom "Home Page"

MUSIC <u>Mr. Raines</u> **MUSIC**

Ashley	Benjamin	Brenda	Caleb
Daris	Eliana	Elias	Esmeralda
George	Homer	Hoss	Isaac
James	Jesse	Jesús	Jill
José	Juan	Luis	Marisela
Mayra	Michael	Patricia	Rebecca A
Rebecca M	Sandra	Secundino	Sergio E
Sergio G	Stacy	Starlene	Andrew

Room 10 at Le Grand Elementary School.
E-mail to Room 10 should include the student's name in both the subject and the body.

Webmaster at Le Grand Elementary School.

THE WORLD WIDE WEB *(cont.)*

WWW SEARCH ENGINES

The following is a list of good search engines to use when trying to find information on the World Wide Web. Some are education specific and others have education areas. Try more than one if you do not locate what you are looking for. Each search engine also has ways for you to register your homepage.

Search for WWW, Usenet Newsgroups, and Gopher Sites

Alta Vista
http://www.altavista.com/

Excite
http://www.excite.com/

HotBot
http://www.hotbot.com/

Infoseek
http://guide.infoseek.com

Lycos
http://www.lycos.com/

Magellan
http://www.mckinley.com/

Yahoo
http://www.yahoo.com/

Other Search Engines on the Web

The Electronic Library
http://www.elibrary.com

Library Clearinghouse
http://www.clearinghouse.net/

Search for e-mail Addresses and Personal Homepages
Four11
http://people.yahoo.com/

WhoWhere
http://www.whowhere.lycos.com/

BigFoot
http://www.bigfoot.com/

Search for Shareware
Shareware.com
http://www.shareware.com

Search Engines for Teachers and Kids
Yahooligans
http://www.yahooligans.com/

Blue N' Web
http://www.kn.pacbell.com/wired/bluewebn/

THE WORLD WIDE WEB *(cont.)*

WEB CREATION RESOURCES

The following is a list of sites to help you with creating your personal, class, or school Web page:

Web Creation Tools

It used to be that in order to create Web pages, you needed to use a programming language called HTML. Although not difficult to learn, many of us do not want to invest the time. Today many software publishers have created web authoring tools as easy to use as a WYSIWYG (what you see is what you get) word processor. In fact many word processors are being marketed now that also author web pages in this way. The following is a list of just such tools:

Software: *Home Page*
Producer: Claris Corporation
URL:
http://www.filemaker.com/products.home page3.html

Software: *PageMill*
Producer: Adobe Corporation
URL:
http://www.adobe.com/prodindex/pagemill/main.html

Software: *BBEdit*
Producer: Barebones
URL: http://www.barebones.com/

Software: *Netscape Navigator Gold*
Producer: Netscape Communications Corporation
URL: http://home.netscape.com

Software: *FrontPage*
Producer: Microsoft
URL:
http://www.microsoft.com/frontpage/default.htm

Software: *HotDog Pro*
Producer: Sausage Software
URL: http://www.sausage.com/

Software: *Kenn Nesbitt's WebEdit*
Producer: Nesbitt Software
URL: http://www.arachne.net/

Software: *HTMLedInternet*
Producer: Software Technologies
URL: http://www.ist.ca/htmled

Software: *AOLpress*
Producer: America Online, Inc.
URL: http://www.aol.com/

THE WORLD WIDE WEB *(cont.)*

Web Creation Tutors

There are several places on the Web to find out how to author for the Web. Here are a few:

Web66

http://www.ncsa.uiuc.edu/General/Internet/WWW/HTMLPrimer.html
Apple Computer
http://www.apple.com/publishing/internet/

Page Templates and Free Graphics

You do not have to be an expert at design and layout, like all those neat little buttons, bullets, icons, lines, and animated goodies that are on Web pages. Just download them and insert your text and graphics and your done. All the resources you will ever need are at Yahoo's WWW directory.

Yahoo's Directory

http://dir.yahoo.com/Computers_and_Internet/Internet?World_Wide_Web/
Page_Creation?

INTEGRATING THE INTERNET INTO THE CURRICULUM

There is so much information on the Internet, making the connection between this technology is more of a joy than a chore. The Internet can make your job more efficient and creative. However, you should be aware, just like the first time you picked up a pencil to write, using technology tools can be awkward and slow at first. Do not give up. As you learn the in's and out's of the Internet, you will find that it can make your teaching more pleasurable.

STEPS TO INTEGRATING THE INTERNET INTO YOUR LESSON PLANS

1. Find an Internet site that is related to your curriculum. This can be easily done by using one of the many search engines available on the Web. (See Search Engines, page 57.)

2. Think about the lessons that you teach within your units of study. Search through the sites to find appropriate sites that enhance your lessons. There are several kinds of sites that can benefit you and your students in different ways. Some are listed below:

   Internet Research: Those sites that are not necessarily written for K-12 education, but might have media and/or research that can be used in kid's projects or as visual aids in your lessons (e.g., The Electronic Zoo on page 155 and The Seven Wonders of the World on page 207).

   Internet Projects: Sites which are dedicated to providing students with activities in which to collaborate with other students all over the world (e.g., GlobaLearn on page 225 and Math Magic on page 189).

   Virtual Field Trips: Taking part in the adventures in which students communicate with experts in the field (e.g., The JASON Project on page 157 and Adventure Online on page 205).

   Publishing on the Internet: Sites that publish student projects for the whole world to see (e.g., Web66 on page 114 and The Poetry Corner on page 236).

   Internet Related and Non-Internet Related Lesson Plans: Several organizations publish lesson plans on the Internet. A lot of these integrate curriculum with technology tools, others are simply good non-technology related lesson plans (e.g., ERIC on page 141 and You Can with Beakman and Jax on page 165).

INTEGRATING THE INTERNET INTO THE CURRICULUM *(cont.)*

3. Implement the lessons at your comfort level. It might be best to use the Internet as a resource for yourself at first. Gathering media and lesson plans is not difficult but the Virtual Field Trips, Publishing, and Projects require more effort. Once you are comfortable with the Internet, you will find that these more interactive type activities are very enjoyable and educational.

The most important thing to remember is that this new media is nothing but a tool for you to use. It is not the tool you use, but how you choose to use the tool.

Some examples of lesson plans are provided for your use starting on page 62 and continuing through page 106.

BOOK REVIEWS FOR THE WORLD TO SEE

Grade Level: 4–8
Content Area: Language Arts, Literature
Skills and Concepts: evaluation, reading

HARDWARE:

an IBM, Macintosh, or compatible computer with an Internet connection

SOFTWARE:

either a Web browsing program such as *Netscape* or *Internet Explorer* or a commercial online account that supports the World Wide Web

OTHER MATERIALS:

one copy of Book Notes for each student, page 63

SUMMARY:

Students will write a book review or report and publish it on the World Wide Web.

BEFORE THE LESSON:

Using a web browsing program open the URL for Book Nook at http://schoolnet2.carleton.ca/english/arts/lit/booknook/index.html. Have your students read reviews of several books at their reading level. Spend time evaluating what makes a good book review. Tell your students that they will be publishing their book reviews at this site. Have your students read a book for the review. They can pick a book from the list of suggestions at the site or choose their own book.

PROCEDURE:

1. Have your students fill in the information on the Book Notes sheet.
2. Using the Book Notes sheet as a guide, have your students write a summary of the book's characters, setting, plot and conclusion. Then have them write an evaluation of the book. Some things that your students could evaluate might be the plot, character development, readability, cover, etc.
3. Edit the writing so that it is clear and free of mistakes.
4. Follow the directions that are at the site for submission of the review.

EXTENSION ACTIVITIES:

- Have students check back after a few days to find their reviews at the site.
- Send notes home to announce the fact that your class has been published on the WWW. Be sure to let everyone know the URL of the site.

BOOK REVIEWS FOR THE WORLD TO SEE

(cont.)

Name: _____   Date: _____

BOOK NOTES

Directions: Fill in all the information on this sheet. It will help you write your review.

Name of the book: _____

Name of the author: _____

Name of the illustrator: _____

Publishing company: _____

List of characters: _____

Describe the setting: _____

Summarize the plot: _____

Did the author do a good job describing the characters? Why or why not?

_____

Did the author do a good job describing the setting? Why or why not? _____

_____

Was the plot enjoyable? Did you enjoy reading the book? _____

_____

Did you like how the book ended? Why or why not? _____

_____

Rate the following on a scale of 1 to 10.

Cover	_____	Characters	_____
Illustrations	_____	Setting	_____
Readability	_____	Plot	_____
Conclusion	_____	Overall Score	_____

HOW'S THE WEATHER?

Grade Level: 4–8

Content Area: Science, Language Arts

Skills and Concepts: observation, making a hypothesis, analyzing, descriptive writing

HARDWARE:

an IBM, Macintosh, or compatible computer with an Internet connection

SOFTWARE:

either a Web browsing program such as *Netscape* or *Internet Explorer* or a commercial online account that supports the World Wide Web

OTHER MATERIALS:

- How's the Weather? Task Sheet, page 66
- How's the Weather? Map, page 67

SUMMARY:

Students will look at a series of weather satellite images in order to make a hypothesis about the direction that weather patterns move in the United States.

BEFORE THE LESSON:

Using a web browsing program open the URL for The Space Science and Engineering Center (SSEC) at http://www.ssec.wisc.edu/data/index.html#sst and use the task card to duplicate what your students will be doing. These sites change periodically, so you may have to update the task card. There are satellite images of the United States in 12 hour intervals. Open each by clicking the corresponding hotlinks (colored words that act like buttons). Make a bookmark for the site so that students can easily navigate there. In most web browsers this is done by going to the BOOKMARK menu and selecting Add a Bookmark. The bookmark now appears in the bookmark menu.

HOW'S THE WEATHER? *(cont.)*

PROCEDURE:

1. Team your students in pairs to complete the lesson.

2. Tell your students that they will be looking at pictures of the United States taken from a weather satellite and will be making a hypothesis about the patterns of weather in the United States. Which way do storms usually move? Can we predict where a storm is going?

3. Tell your students that they need to follow the directions on the task card very carefully.

4. Pass out the task cards and maps to your class. Have students go to the computer and complete the assignment.

EXTENSION ACTIVITIES:

• Check the satellite images over several days to track storms as they move.

• Have students do a videotaped weather forecast. Bring up the images on the computer screen or large screen projection device and position the video camera so that both the screen and the student can be seen. Have the student explain the weather patterns.

HOW'S THE WEATHER? *(cont.)*

HOW'S THE WEATHER? TASK SHEET

Name(s):_____ Date: _____

1. Make an Internet connection and start the Web browsing program.

2. Go to the BOOKMARK menu and select The Space Science and Engineering Center (SSEC) bookmark. The connection may take a few minutes to complete.

3. Click on the hotlink (colored word) for the 36-hour satellite image. This is a picture of the United States from a satellite within the last 36 hours.

4. With a blue crayon or pencil, copy the outline of the cloud pattern shown on the screen to your map. Use the states as a guide and be as accurate as you can.

5. Click the Back button at the top of the screen. This will take you back to the last screen.

6. Click the hotlink for the 24-hour satellite image. This is a satellite picture of the United States 12 hours after the first picture.

7. With a green crayon repeat step 4 using the 24-hour image as a guide. Use your pencil to draw arrows in the direction the clouds seem to be moving.

8. Click the Back button at the top of the screen. This will take you back to the last screen.

9. Click the hotlink for the 12-hour satellite image. This is a satellite picture of the United States 12 hours after the second picture.

10. With a blue crayon repeat step 4 using the 12-hour image as a guide. Use your pencil to draw arrows in the direction the clouds seem to be moving.

11. Quit the Web browsing program and close your Internet connection.

12. Complete the questions on the bottom of the How's the Weather Map page.

HOW'S THE WEATHER? *(cont.)*

HOW'S THE WEATHER? MAP

Directions: Follow the procedure on the How's the Weather? Task Sheet to complete the map of the United States and then answer the questions at the bottom of the page.

Questions:

1. Describe the changes in the cloud patterns.
2. Was there a pattern in the way in which storms moved across the United States? If so, what was it?
3. Can you think of any reason that the storms might move in this direction?

CITIZENSHIP

Grade Level: 5–8

Content Area: Social Studies

Skills and Concepts: using the Internet, multi-culturalism, communication, consensus, task organization

HARDWARE:
- an IBM, Macintosh, or compatible computer with a connection to the Internet
- a large screen projection device

SOFTWARE:
either a Web browsing program such as *Netscape* or *Internet Explorer* or a commercial on-line account that supports the World Wide Web

TCM Resource Book: *Cooperative Learning Activities for Social Studies* (TCM 655)

OTHER MATERIALS:
- one copy per student of Requirements for Citizenship, page 70
- one copy per student of Citizenship Guide, page 71
- one copy per student of Citizenship Award, page 72

SUMMARY:
Students will research the requirements for United States citizenship and create requirements for their group citizenship.

BEFORE THE LESSON:
Use the program to locate the FedWorld homepage at http://www.fedworld.gov. Use the search button to search for "citizenship requirements". This will take you to a document that contains text describing the requirements and process for becoming a United States citizen.

PROCEDURE:
1. Divide your students into groups of four to six and lead them in a discussion of the idea of citizenship and what it means to be a citizen of the United States. Ask them if they know what is required to become a United States citizen.

CITIZENSHIP *(cont.)*

PROCEDURE *(cont.)*

2. Research the requirements for becoming a United States citizen. Using a large screen projection device, project the information found on FedWorld to discuss the requirements for citizenship. If you wish groups to find the information themselves, teach them how to locate and print the information.

3. Using Requirements for Citizenship, page 70, have the groups write the requirements for being citizens of their group. Tell them to remember that each of them must be able to pass the requirements that they make up.

4. Have the group write their requirements into a Citizenship Guide, page 71.

5. Have each member attempt to pass the requirements of citizenship. Give out Citizenship Awards, page 72, for those who pass.

EXTENSION ACTIVITIES:

- Use the FedWorld homepage as a starting point for research on the different offices of the cabinet.

- Have your students find out what each cabinet office does.

- Have your students explore FedWorld and evaluate its effectiveness at informing the public.

CITIZENSHIP *(cont.)*

REQUIREMENTS FOR CITIZENSHIP

You are going to plan requirements for citizenship within your group. Here are the three steps you need to take:

First, discuss the requirements for citizenship within your group, and write the four requirements for citizenship on the Citizenship Guide page.

Next, each person in your group must fulfill the requirements for citizenship.

After your group has become citizens, join your class for a citizenship celebration.

❑ What are some of the things that you feel are important requirments to become citizens of your group?

_____

❑ What will citizens have to know? (a pledge, a song, something about history or laws)

_____

❑ What will citizens have to promise? (to protect and defend the Constitution, etc.)

_____

❑ Will citizens have to take a test? If so, what will it cover?

_____

❑ Will citizens have to prove anything? If so, what?

_____

❑ Notes:

_____

_____

_____

_____

CITIZENSHIP *(cont.)*

CITIZENSHIP GUIDE

1. You must know . . .

2. You must promise . . .

3. You must be tested on or for . . .

4. You must prove . . .

CITIZENSHIP *(cont.)*

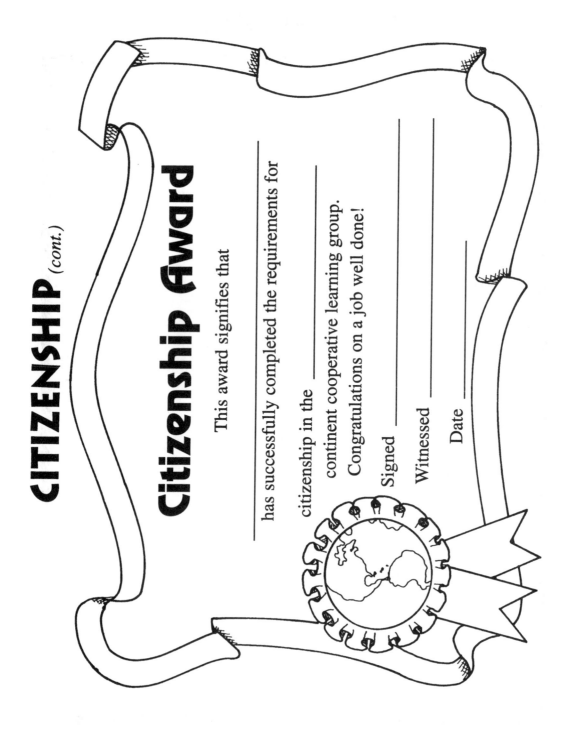

Citizenship Award

This award signifies that

_____

has successfully completed the requirements for

citizenship in the _____

continent cooperative learning group.

Congratulations on a job well done!

Signed _____

Witnessed _____

Date _____

SHAKESPEARE

Grade Level: 8

Content Area: Literature

Skills and Concepts: using the Internet WWW site, interpreting *Shakespeare*

HARDWARE:

- an IBM, Macintosh, or compatible computer with a connection to the Internet
- a large screen projection device, optional

SOFTWARE:

either a Web browsing program such as *Netscape* or *Internet Explorer* or a commercial online account that supports the World Wide Web

TCM Resource Book: *Shakespeare* (TCM 614)

OTHER MATERIALS:

one page per student of Responses, page 74

SUMMARY:

This is a lesson that would go with a unit on Shakespeare's *Romeo and Juliet*. In this lesson your students explore *The Complete Works of Shakespeare* homepage on the World Wide Web to determine the meanings of quotes.

BEFORE THE LESSON:

Explore *The Complete Works of Shakespeare* homepage (http://the-tech.mit.edu/Shakespeare/works.html) to become familiar with navigating through the page.

PROCEDURE:

1. Explain to your students that they will be using an online version of *Romeo and Juliet* to help them find out meanings for some important quotations in the story.
2. Hand out the Responses worksheet on page 74 and read the quotes together. Have your students try to interpret the meanings out of context.
3. Click the link to *Romeo and Juliet* then explore the online book in search of the quotes.

Note: If your school is using a dial-up connection it may be impossible or too costly to use the pod or lab configurations for this lesson. Direct-connect schools will have no problems as there is no charge for the time online in most cases.

EXTENSION ACTIVITIES:

- Have your students enter the quotation area of the Shakespeare page and find familiar quotes. Then, have them analyze why these quotes have stood the test of time and are still used today..

SHAKESPEARE *(cont.)*

RESPONSES

Explain the meanings of the following quotations from *Romeo and Juliet*.

1. "Down with the Capulets! Down with the Montagues!"

   _____

   _____

2. "Oh speak again, bright angel! For thou art
   As glorious to this night, being o'er my head
   As is a winged messenger of Heaven."

   _____

   _____

3. "Never was seen so black a day as this.
   Oh, woeful day, oh, woeful day!"

   _____

   _____

4. "Hold, there is forty ducats. Let me have a dram of poison."

   _____

   _____

5. "Take him and cut him out in little stars,
   And he will make the face of heaven so fine
   That all the world will be in love with night."

   _____

   _____

6. "Come, come with me, and we will make short work,
   For, by your leaves, you shall not stay alone
   Till Holy Church incorporate two in one."

   _____

   _____

POETRY ON THE NET

Grade Level: Any

Content Area: Literature

Skills and Concepts: using the Internet WWW site, writing haiku poetry, publishing work on the Internet

HARDWARE:

- an IBM, Macintosh, or compatible computer with a connection to the Internet
- a large screen projection device, optional

SOFTWARE:

- either a Web browsing program such as *Netscape* or *Internet Explorer* a commercial online account that supports the World Wide Web
- a word processing program

TCM Resource Book: *I Can Write a Poem* (TCM 326)

OTHER MATERIALS:

one copy per student of Haiku, pages 77 and 78

SUMMARY:

Students will write Haiku poems that will be published on the Internet for people all over the world to see.

BEFORE THE LESSON:

Explore The Poetry Corner homepage (http://www.virtualnevada.com/orphanedthoughts.htm) to become familiar with navigating through the page and submitting work.

PROCEDURE:

1. If available, use a large screen projection device to show the class The Poetry Corner homepage. Move through the page looking for samples of student work that may be of interest to the class. Tell them that they will be writing poetry that will be submitted to this page so that other students all over the world can see it. Tell them that they can even get letters via e-mail from people who want to ask questions about their poem.

POETRY ON THE NET *(cont.)*

PROCEDURE *(cont.)*

2. Teach your students the form of the poetry you wish them to write. A handout for Haiku is included for your use, but any form of poetry can be submitted. Have your students write their poems.

3. Revise, edit, and rewrite the poems using a word processing program. Be sure to include the name of the author and an e-mail address, if you have one. It is important that the final product be saved as a text file so that it can be easily submitted. Read the manual for your software to find out how this is done. Many times the file formats can be changed with the Save As command.

4. All the poems can be submitted at one time using one computer. Simply click the Submit button at The Poetry Corner homepage and follow the directions.

5. Revisit the homepage in about a week and find your submissions.

EXTENSION ACTIVITIES:

Write an author of a poem you enjoyed reading. Ask where they got their inspiration or what their process was for writing it.

POETRY ON THE NET *(cont.)*

HAIKU

 1 2 3   4 5
Japanese Haiku   5

   1   2 3 4 5 6   7
Captures a moment in time   7

   1   2   3 4 5
Snapshot memory.   5

Haiku has no rhyme   5

But has a special structure 7

To create within.   5

Each poem has three lines   5

With seventeen syllables   7

In five, seven, five.   5

When you write Haiku   5

Remember, freeze a moment, 7

Let it live in words.   5

Mark the syllables in the Haiku above. The first one is done for you. When you write Haiku, remember to "freeze" a moment. Here is an examle.

Wind, gently blowing
Up, around, and through the trees,
Plays tag with my kite.

Write a definition of Haiku. _____

_____

POETRY ON THE NET *(cont.)*

HAIKU

Now it's your turn to write Haiku!
Remember to count the syllables carefully.
Make a list of ten words to describe Spring and how you feel about Spring.

_____ _____ _____ _____ _____

_____ _____ _____ _____ _____

Use some of these words and ideas to finish this Haiku about Spring.

1 2 3   4   5
Opening blossoms _____ 5

_____ 7

_____ 5

Write the first two lines for this Haiku about a puppy.

_____ 5

_____ 7

 1   2   3   4   5
Chews on my new shoe! _____ 5

Write a Haiku about your favorite sport.

_____ 5

_____ 7

_____ 5

Write a Haiku using one of your own ideas for a subject.

_____ 5

_____ 7

_____ 5

DRAWING THE LINE

Grade Level: 7–8

Content Area: Geography, Social Studies

Skills and Concepts: using the Internet WWW site, physical and political geography, supporting a hypothesis

HARDWARE:

- an IBM, Macintosh, or compatible computer with a connection to the Internet
- a large screen projection device, optional

SOFTWARE:

- either a Web browsing program such as *Netscape* or *Internet Explorer* or a commercial online account that supports the World Wide Web
- a word processing program

TCM Resource Book: *Colonial America* (TCM 597)

OTHER MATERIALS:

- one copy per student of Drawing the Line, page 81
- one copy per student of page 82
- one green, red, blue, and brown colored pencil for each student

SUMMARY:

Using an online interactive map of the United States your students will see how physical geography shaped the formation of the political boundaries of the original thirteen colonies.

BEFORE THE LESSON:

Spend some time exploring the interactive color relief map (http://www.nationalgeographic.com/maps/physical.html). When you first arrive at the site you are greeted by a color relief map of the United States with a grid superimposed. Click inside any of the squares to get a close up view. Do the worksheet yourself to anticipate any problems that your class may have. If you have a large screen projection device, have it ready before this lesson.

DRAWING THE LINE *(cont.)*

PROCEDURE:

1. Ask your class if they know why the boundaries of the original thirteen colonies are where they are. Take all responses, then ask if they think the physical geography had anything to do with the boundaries. Tell them that they will be using an online interactive map that was made by NASA using a satellite to see if geography might have had something to do with the borders.

2. Complete the activity sheets. Make your connection to the Web site and display the map on a large screen projection device. Start with the New England states by clicking the grid area that corresponds with them. You will zoom in on the area to reveal a detailed physical map. Have your students fill out the map and handout. Repeat this step, moving through each of the colonies.

3. Ask students to share the results of their work. Ask if they think that geography shaped some of the boundaries of the original colonies. Ask which ones seem to be most effected by geography and why they were effected.

Note: In grading this assignment, you should not be concerned with the hypothesis your students make. The assignment should be graded on how well your students supported their hypothesis.

EXTENSION ACTIVITIES:

- Save the maps found as picture files for published reports or stories. In most web browsing programs you do this by simply holding the mouse button down while pointing at the picture, then select Save from the FILE menu.

- Repeat this activity for the state in which you live. Did geography shape the boundaries of your state?

DRAWING THE LINE *(cont.)*

Name(s):_____ Date: _____

Directions: Did physical geography (what the land is like) help to shape the boundaries of the thirteen original colonies? Use an interactive physical map to find out.

1. Look at the interactive map of the thirteen original colonies. Then use the following color key to indicate each land form that might have effected the boundary.

   red = river

   blue = ocean or lake

   green = valley

   brown = mountains

2. In the following chart, explain how physical geography has effected the boundaries of the colonies. Remember to use cardinal directions to describe the border (e.g., the western border of Pennsylvania).

State Name	Border Effected (use directions)	What geographical features do you believe affected the border?

DRAWING THE LINE *(cont.)*

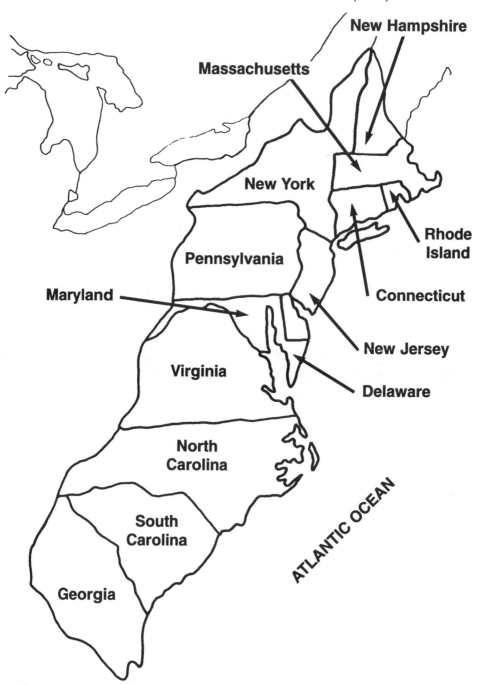

New Hampshire

Massachusetts

New York

Pennsylvania

Rhode Island

Maryland

Connecticut

Virginia

New Jersey

Delaware

North Carolina

ATLANTIC OCEAN

South Carolina

Georgia

WHERE IN THE WORLD AM I?

Grade Level: 3 and up

Content Area: Social Studies, Language Arts

Skills and Concepts: geography, research and communications

HARDWARE:

an IBM, Macintosh, or compatible computer with a connection to the Internet

SOFTWARE:

either a Web browsing program such as *Netscape* or *Internet Explorer* or a commercial online account that supports the World Wide Web

OTHER MATERIALS:

- Where in the World Am I? Clue Sheet, page 85
- World Map, page 86
- United States Map, page 87

SUMMARY:

Students will send and receive clues from students from around the world about where they are located (e.g., country, state, area, city, etc.). Both sets of students will use these clues to guess their whereabouts.

BEFORE THE LESSON:

Make a call for collaboration with another class or classes. Good places to find classes include the following:

- Kidsphere Listserv (See Listservs, pages 29-32.), subscribe by sending an e-mail to: kidsphere-request@vms.cis.pitt.edu. Once you have been added to the Listserv, call for collaboration by sending an e-mail describing the project to kidsphere@vms.cis.pitt.edu. Make sure you give classes a deadline for getting back to you.

- The Electronic SchoolNet has a more formal project similar to this called Geography Detectives. You can find it on the web at http://www.gsn.org.

WHERE IN THE WORLD AM I? *(cont.)*

PROCEDURE:

1. Have students research their state, area, and city. Fill in the information on the Where in the World Am I? Clue Sheet. Check the clues for accuracy.

2. E-mail one clue per day to the participating classes/students.

3. Receive your clues, print them out, and work on them in class. Provide students with atlases and other reference materials to search. Have your students make notes on the World and United States maps that help them narrow the search. Circle areas that are suspect with different color markers as per the directions on the maps.

4. E-mail guesses and review your partner class's guesses. Try to narrow down the search from large to small, for example, country to state to area to city.

EXTENSION ACTIVITIES:

- Have your students become keypals with your partner class.

- When you are finished with the project, pretend that you moved to somewhere else in the world and do the project again with the same class.

WHERE IN THE WORLD AM I? *(cont.)*

Name(s): _____ Date: _____

WHERE IN THE WORLD AM I? CLUE SHEET

Country Clues:

Colors of Flag: _____

National Symbol: _____

Famous for: _____

Famous Leader: _____

Hemisphere: _____

Other: _____

State or Area Clues:

Famous Person (People) from the Area: _____

Famous Tourist Attraction(s):_____

Chief Products:_____

Major Geographic Landforms:_____

Other: _____

City or Town Clues:

Longitude: _____

Latitude: _____

If Not a Major City, Closest Major City:_____

Population: _____

Other: _____

WHERE IN THE WORLD AM I? *(cont.)*

WHERE IN THE WORLD AM I? WORLD CLUE MAP

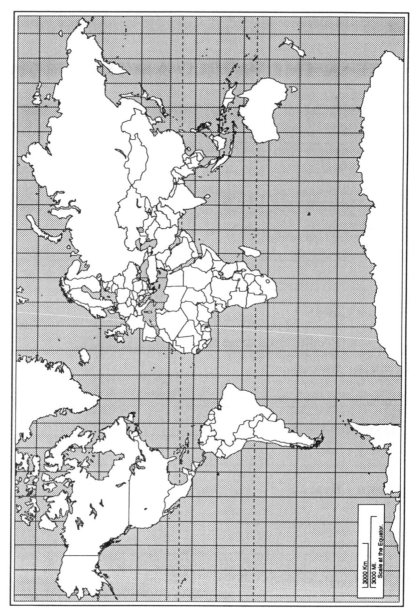

Directions: Each day that you receive a clue from your partner class, draw circles and make notes on the map to indicate where you think they may be. Use a different color marker or crayon for each day.

WHERE IN THE WORLD AM I? *(cont.)*

WHERE IN THE WORLD AM I? U.S. CLUE MAP

Directions: Each day that you receive a clue from your partner class, draw circles and make notes on the map to indicate where you think they may be. Use a different color marker or crayon for each day.

LET'S TAKE A VIRTUAL TOUR

Grade Level: 5 and up

Content Area: Social Studies, Language Arts

Skills and Concepts: geography, research, and communications

HARDWARE:

an IBM, Macintosh, or compatible computer with a connection to the Internet

SOFTWARE:

either a Web browsing program such as *Netscape* or *Internet Explorer* or a commercial online account that supports the World Wide Web

OTHER MATERIALS:

- World Map, page 90
- Travel Log, page 91 (one page for each student for each city that they will visit or each day of their trip.)

SUMMARY:

Students will virtually tour several major cities of the world, collecting information from each.

BEFORE THE LESSON:

Teach students how to navigate through web pages using a mouse. Make sure they understand the back command and know how to see a summary of their movements. This is located in the GO menu in *Netscape*. Explore the Virtual Tourist Site at http://www.vtourist.com

PROCEDURE:

1. Give each student a map of the world. Tell them that they will be going on a virtual tour of world cities using the Internent. Before giving the maps to your students, list all of the cities you want them to travel to on their maps. This will, of course, depend on the amount of time each student is allotted.

2. Have them trace their route from the approximate position of their city through other cities to which they wish to travel.

LET'S TAKE A VIRTUAL TOUR *(cont.)*

PROCEDURE *(cont.)*

3. Have them log onto the virtual tourist site (http://www.vtourist.com) and access the information for each city. Have them fill out the information in their Travel Log.

EXTENSION ACTIVITIES:

- Have your students report to the class about their favorite city.
- Have each student e-mail the tourism department of the city that they visit to ask for pamphlets or travel brochures.
- Create a computerized travel log with pictures collected from web pages that your students visit. Pictures can be collected by holding the mouse button down while the cursor is on the picture. Select Save As from the drop down window, name the picture, pick a directory or disk to store it in, and click save. The picture can now be used in most word processors. (See your word processor's documentation to find out how to insert pictures and if it supports GIF and JPEG file recognition. These are how pictures from the web are saved.)
- If you are studying a particular country, you may want to have your students do a virtual tour of just that country.

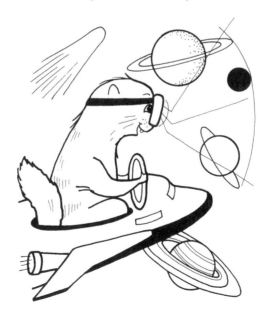

LET'S TAKE A VIRTUAL TOUR *(cont.)*

VIRTUAL TOUR WORLD MAP

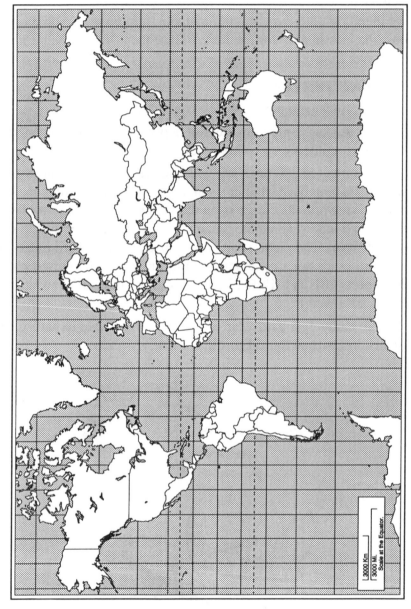

Directions: Using a pencil, trace the route from the approximate position of your city through other cities in which you wish to travel on your virtual tour.

LET'S TAKE A VIRTUAL TOUR *(cont.)*

VIRTUAL TOUR TRAVEL LOG

Travel Log for: _____ Date: _____

Day number _____ of my trip.

Destination City: _____ Country: _____

Write the names and descriptions of things that you saw on your tour.

_____

_____

_____

_____

What were some interesting facts that you learned about the city that
you visited?

_____

_____

_____

_____

Would you recommend this city to a friend who is thinking of going there?
Why or why not?

_____

_____

_____

_____

SURFING FOR INFORMATION

Grade Level: 4 and up

Content Area: Any

Skills and Concepts: learning content, using the Internet as a research tool

HARDWARE:

an IBM, Macintosh, or compatible computer with a connection to the Internet

SOFTWARE:

either a Web browsing program such as *Netscape* or *Internet Explorer* or a commercial online account that supports the World Wide Web

OTHER MATERIALS:

Surf Research, page 94 (one per student per subtopic)

SUMMARY:

Students will research a subject that you assign by using the Internet and search engines.

BEFORE THE LESSON:

Make yourself familiar with one of the following search engines so that you can teach the skills necessary for your students to use them. (See Search Engines, page 57.) Choose a subject that you are covering in class to research.

Alta Vista
http://www.altavista.com

Excite
http://www.excite.com/

Infoseek
http://guide.infoseek.com

Lycos
http://www.lycos.com/

Magellan
http://www.mckinley.com/

Yahoo
http://www.yahoo.com/

SURFING FOR INFORMATION *(cont.)*

PROCEDURE:

1. Talk about the subject that you have been covering in class. Tell your class that they are going to use the Internet to research information about a topic related to the subject. Brainstorm or assign topics to your students.

2. Have your students think of several subtopics that they will cover about the topic, for example, Topic: bears. Subtopics: environment, feeding habits, behavior.

3. Allow students to research their topics using a search engine to find the information.

Note: Make sure that computers have blocking software like *NetNanny* or *Cyber Patrol* and that you monitor students who are using the Internet. Keywords that are entered by students may have several meanings, some of them inappropriate. Remember, search engines have no mind of their own. They will return with a list of all the sites that include the keyword, whatever its intended meaning.

EXTENSION ACTIVITIES:

- Print out Web documents that contain information that can be used often. Create a file of these and include the URL of the site.

- Teach your students how to cite electronic resources.

SURFING FOR INFORMATION *(cont.)*

SURF RESEARCH

Name: _____ Date: _____

Directions: Use an Internet search engine to find information about your topic. Make sure that you focus on the subtopics. Print the information that covers the topic that you need.

I. Topic: _____

Subtopics:

A. _____

B. _____

C. _____

D. _____

I will use _____ as my search engine(s) to find sites about my topic.

Internet Sites Used:

Name of the Site	Type of Site*	URL of the Site
*WWW, Gopher, or FTP		

KEYPALS

Grade Level: 3 and up

Content Area: Language Arts

Skills and Concepts: writing a friendly letter, using e-mail

HARDWARE:

an IBM, Macintosh, or compatible computer with a connection to the Internet

SOFTWARE:

either a Web browsing program such as *Netscape* or *Internet Explorer* or a commercial online account that supports the World Wide Web

- e-mail software (included in many browsers)

OTHER MATERIALS:

Let Me Introduce Myself, page 97

SUMMARY:

Students will introduce themselves to national or international keypals using e-mail.

BEFORE THE LESSON:

Make a call for keypals with another class or classes. These can be in the same class or different classes. Good places to find classes include the following:

- Kidsphere Listserv (See Listservs, pages 29-32.)

  Subscribe by sending an e-mail to: kidsphere-request@vms.cis.pitt.edu.

  Once you have been added to the Listserv call for collaboration by sending an e-mail describing the project to kidsphere@vms.cis.pitt.edu. Make sure you give classes a deadline for getting back to you.

- Intercultural E-mail Classroom Connections (http://www.stolaf.edu/network/iecc/) has a system for setting up keypals from different parts of the world.

Correspond with the teacher of the class as to how and when the exchange will be made. Will you send text attached to an e-mail or will each student send an e-mail? This will depend on your school's student access to e-mail accounts.

KEYPALS *(cont.)*

PROCEDURE:

1. Spend some time learning about the class that you have chosen for keypals. Assign a keypal to each student or wait until after this assignment to assign students of similar interests.

2. Have your students use the Let Me Introduce Myself page to help them think about things that they can say about themselves.

3. Using the Let Me Introduce Myself page, have your students type and edit their letters of introduction to their keypals. This may be done directly into an e-mail message or into a word processor depending on what you and the other teacher have decided upon.

4. Send the e-mail and wait for a reply.

EXTENSION ACTIVITIES:

- Work on collaborative projects with keypals such as comparing and contrasting cultures, science experiments that deal with variables from both areas, or a joint history report.

- Send a video or photographic journal of your school starring your class.

- Use video conferencing software to have a live chat with your keypals. Use a search engine to find out more information on using CU-SEEME or other video conferencing software at your school.

KEYPALS *(cont.)*

LET ME INTRODUCE MYSELF

Name: _____ Date: _____

Directions: Fill in the following information. It will help you write your introduction letter to your keypal.

About Me

Age: ____ Height: _____ Hair Color: _____ Eye Color: _____

Birthday: _____

My favorite things: _____

_____

What I like to do: _____

_____

My favorite subject in school: _____

_____

About My Family

Parents' names: _____

Sisters' and brothers' names: _____

Things we do together: _____

Places we like to go: _____

Our house: _____

Our Pets: _____

About My School

School Name: _____

Mascot: _____

Teacher's Name(s) _____

Our day: _____

My favorite thing about school: _____

Other Things About Me

ARE ALL SCHOOLS THE SAME?

Grade Level: 3 and up

Content Area: Language Arts

Skills and Concepts: comparing and contrasting, geographic regions

HARDWARE:

an IBM, Macintosh, or compatible computer with a connection to the Internet

SOFTWARE:

- either a Web browsing program such as *Netscape* or *Internet Explorer* or a commercial online account that supports the World Wide Web

- e-mail software (included in many browsers)

OTHER MATERIALS:

- School Information Sheet, page 100
- Are All Schools the Same? Venn diagram, page 101

SUMMARY:

Students will use the Internet to gather information about other schools in two different geographic regions of the United States. They will use this information to compare and contrast major elements of their school with that of the other schools.

BEFORE THE LESSON:

Access the International Schools Registry (http://web66.coled.umn.edu/schools.html) or the Hotlist of K-12 Internet School Sites (http://www.gsn.org/hotlist.index.html) and tour around schools in three distinctly different geographic regions of the United States. Teach students how to access one of the sites listed above. Be prepared to divide your class into teams of two.

PROCEDURE:

1. Ask students if they think that all schools are the same. Take all their responses. Ask them if they think that schools in different parts of the United States are the same.

ARE ALL SCHOOLS THE SAME? *(cont.)*

PROCEDURE *(cont.)*

2. Use the Schools Information Sheet to fill in information about your school

3. Tell your students they are going to be using the Internet to find out this same information about other schools in different geographic regions of the United States.

4. Discuss what regions are and which states might be in different geographic regions other than your school.

5. Divide your class into teams of two and have them decide on two different regions that they will search for schools in.

6. Have each student in the team take a different region and use one of the hotlists above to find a school in that region that has all the information needed on their web page. They will probably have to call, mail, or e-mail the school for the information that is not included in the web site. Use the School Information Sheet to gather the information.

7. Have your student teams fill out the three-way Venn diagram and discuss the comparison.

EXTENSION ACTIVITIES:

• Scan the Venn diagrams and send them with each team's written analysis to schools that you compared.

• Evaluate other schools' web sites and start designing your own.

ARE ALL SCHOOLS THE SAME? *(cont.)*

SCHOOL INFORMATION SHEET

Name(s):_____Date: _____

School Name: _____

Address: _____

City: _____ State: _____

Region of the U.S.: _____

E-mail Address: _____

URL of Web Page:_____

Student population: _____ Teacher Population: _____

Grade Levels: _____

What is the class schedule?_____

_____

What does our grade level study in Math? _____

_____

Language Arts? _____

_____

Social Studies?_____

_____

Science?_____

_____

What is physical education like?_____

100

ARE ALL SCHOOLS THE SAME? *(cont.)*

Directions: Use the Venn diagram to compare the three schools that you researched.

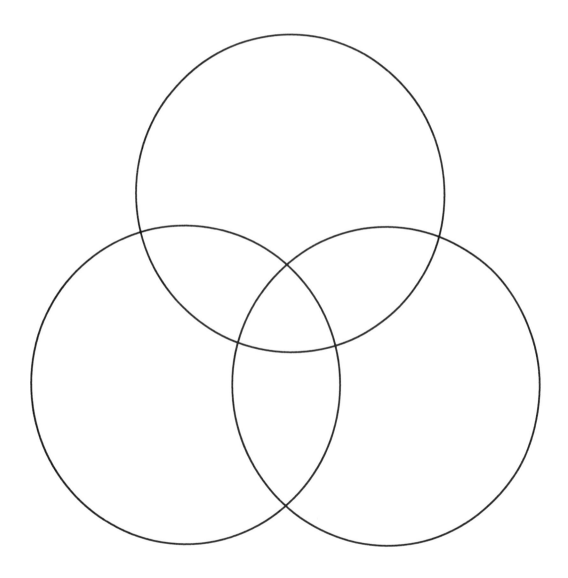

KID NEWS

Grade Level: 4 and up

Content Area: Language Arts

Skills and Concepts: writing a news story

HARDWARE:

an IBM, Macintosh, or compatible computer with a connection to the Internet

SOFTWARE:

- either a Web browsing program such as *Netscape* or *Internet Explorer* or a commercial online account that supports the World Wide Web

- e-mail software (included in many browsers)

OTHER MATERIALS:

- The News Story, pages 104–106
- current newspaper articles

SUMMARY:

Your students will write a newspaper article that they will submit for publishing on the World Wide Web.

BEFORE THE LESSON:

Explore the KidNews site to find out how to publish students' work at their site. (http://www.vsa.cape.com/~powens/Kidnews3.html). Another good source for newspaper lesson plans is Newspapers in Education (http://www.detnews.com/nie/).

PROCEDURE:

1. Tell your students that they will be writing their own newspaper and publishing it on the Internet.

2. Distribute newspaper articles and copies of Activity 1 (page 104) to your students. Have them read the articles within their groups to find the following information and record it on their work sheets. Allow each group to share its findings with the class.

headline	byline	climax
main idea of the story	dateline	details

KID NEWS *(cont.)*

PROCEDURE *(cont.)*

3. Prepare students for writing a news story by discussing actual news events that might be used for their articles or choose an imaginary incident from the following: car crash, fire, arrival of a prominent person, football game, earthquake, or another type of natural disaster.

4. Allow students to draw pictures of the event.

5. Discuss and list on a chart or chalkboard good lead lines, such as the following:

Quote Example— "The earth shook like a bowl of jelly," exclaimed the woman as she stood by her devastated home after the earthquake.

Dramatic Word Picture Example—The ground trembled, houses shook, and trees swayed back and forth as the earthquake shook the city of San Francisco.

Summary Stating the Facts—The death toll is yet unknown, but the amount of damage caused by the earthquake that struck San Francisco is estimated to be in the millions of dollars.

Question Example—What caused such a devastating fire? Firemen are now investigating the cause of the fire that burned hundreds of homes in the Oakland Hills area yesterday.

6. Reproduce Activity 2 (pages 105 and 106) for students. Have them use the format provided on the work sheets to write their own news stories.

7. Submit the articles to KidNews by following the instructions on their web page (http://www.vsa.cape.com/~powens/Kidnews3.html).

EXTENSION ACTIVITIES:

Have you students follow the same procedure and develop a class magazine to publish on the Internet.

KID NEWS *(cont.)*

Activity 1—Taking Notes

Choose a feature article from the newspaper. After reading the article, practice taking notes about your article by completing the information below. You may wish to refer to this worksheet as a guide for writing your own news story (pages 105–106).

Headline:_____

Main idea of story: _____

_____

Byline: _____

Dateline: _____

Climax:

    Who?_____

    When? _____

    Where? _____

    What? _____

    Why?_____

    How?_____

Details: _____

_____

_____

_____

_____

_____

_____

_____

_____

_____

_____

KID NEWS *(cont.)*

Activity 2—Writing a News Story

Choose an exciting or interesting event that has occurred recently or that you have created in your imagination. Use a separate sheet of paper to make notes about the event. You can use page 104 as a guide. Fill in the important information about this event below and on page 106. Using this information, write the news story in paragraph form.

Headline: _____

Main idea of story: _____

_____

_____

_____

_____

_____

Byline (name of reporter): _____

Dateline (date, city, state): _____

_____

Paragraph 1 (Lead paragraph)

The first sentence is dramatic. This paragraph provides a brief description that gives important information about *who, when, where,* and *what.* Then it explains *why* and *how.*

_____

_____

_____

_____

_____

_____

_____

_____

KID NEWS *(cont.)*

Activity 2—Writing a News Story *(cont.)*

Paragraph 2

This paragraph tells other important information.

_____

_____

_____

_____

_____

_____

Paragraph 3

This paragraph provides additional details. Remember to begin a sentence with a quotation, a dramatic word picture, a summary stating the facts, or a question.

_____

_____

_____

_____

_____

_____

Checklist for a Good News Story

Review the news story you have written, using the checklist shown below. Be sure that you can answer *yes* before you place a check (✓) next to each question.

○ Is my headline clear and interesting?   ○ Are my news sources cited?

○ Is my story organized correctly?   ○ Are direct quotations used?

○ Are my spelling and grammar correct?   ○ Is my story clear?

Name:

Online Educational Resources

URL:

http://quest.arc.nasa.gov/OER/

Description of Site:

Run by NASA's High Performance Computing and Communications program, this site's mission is to foster increased use of new computer and networking technologies to help support accelerated learning programs in education. These rough listings provide pointers to some online resources for students and educators, as well as to projects that address these goals.

What to Do There:

This site points or links to tons of information and ideas for using the Internet in the classroom. Some of the headings include School and Community Networking Resources, NASA Internet Educational Resources, Educational Organizations and Programs, University and College Resources, Resource Lists and Subject Trees on Education, Museums and Expositions Online, Online Libraries, Collaborative Technology Resources, Projects and Datasets, Search Pages, and Resource Discovery Engines.

Name:

Children's Online Literature Gopher

URL:

gopher://lib.nmsu.edu/11/.subjects/Education/.childlit

Description of Site:

Established and maintained by New Mexico State University, this site is a storehouse of information on children's literature. Choose from the following: About Children's Literature: Electronic Resources, Author Information, Awards, Bibliographies, Indexes and Library Guides, Children's Literature Centers and Collections, Children's Literature: A Guide to Criticism (online book), Conferences, Electronic Children's Books, Electronic Journals and Book Reviews, Internet Resources for Children's Literature, Organizations, Papers, Booktalks, Reader's Theater, Professional Journals, Publishers and Bookstores, and Syllabi.

What to Do There:

This is a perfect site to teach reference research. One of the portions of the site is the Reader's Theater. Several books have been converted to reader scripts. They can be printed and used for reading in class.

The Children's Literature Web Guide

Internet Resources Related to Books for Children and Young Adults

Name:

The Children's Literature Web Guide

URL:

http://www.acs.ucalgary.ca/~dkbrown/

Description of Site:

This site includes the following: Movies and Television Based on Children's Books, Children's Book Awards, Best Books Lists, Children's Bestsellers, Resource Links Canadian Bestsellers, Publisher's Weekly Children's Bestsellers (U.S.), Online Children's Stories, Collections, Classics, Folklore, Myth and Legend, Contemporary Stories, Children's Songs and Poetry, Readers' Theater, Written by Children, General Children's Literature Resources, Children's Literature Journals and Book Reviews Online, Internet Discussion Groups, Conferences and Book Events, Related Associations on the Internet, Information about Authors and Their Books, Children's Book Publishers, Children's Booksellers, Digging Deeper, Research Guides and Indexes, Clearinghouse Approved, Resources for Parents, Resources for Teachers, Resources for Storytellers, and Resources for Writers and Illustrators.

What to Do There:

One idea that you can do at this site would be to have students research the authors of the books that they have read. This site has links to information about several popular children's authors. Many of the authors even have e-mail addresses so that students can write to them.

Name:

Odyssey of the Mind

URL:

http://www.odyssey.org/odyssey/

Description of Site:

Odyssey of the Mind is a world wide, nonprofit organization that promotes creative team-based problem solving in school programs for students from kindergarten through college. This program helps students learn divergent thinking and problem solving skills while participating in a series of challenging and motivating activities, both inside and outside their regular classroom curriculum.

What to Do There:

The Odyssey of the Mind School Program fosters creative thinking and problem-solving skills among participating students from kindergarten through college. It features an annual competition component at local through international levels. Students solve problems in a variety of areas—from building mechanical devices such as spring-driven vehicles to giving their own interpretation of literary classics. Through solving problems, students learn life-long skills such as working with others as a team, evaluating ideas, making decisions, and creating solutions while also developing self-confidence from their experiences.

Teaching and Learning on the Web

Name:

Teaching and Learning on the Web

URL:

http://www.mcli.dist.maricopa.edu/tl/

Description of Site:

This searchable collection gives you access to sites that are dedicated to teaching and learning of any kind, not just technology related to learning. Find lesson plans, units, research, and content.

What to Do There:

Great starting place to find anything that has to do with using teaching and learning. Find ideas, lesson plans, projects, publishers, companies, research, anything that has to do with teaching and learning. To use the page, simply type in the subject that you are looking for in the form box provided and click the Go! button. You can even narrow the search with the category menu. Click and hold on the drop down menu, then drag to the category in which you wish the search to be limited.

Name:

Totware—Benjamin's Favorites

URL:

http://www.het.brown.edu/people/mende/totware.html

Description of Site:

This site is loaded with PC and Mac shareware and freeware programs that have been reviewed by the page author's son, Benjamin.

What to Do There:

If you have younger children you will love this site! Download fully functional versions of children's software. All of these are either shareware or freeware. (See page 57.) Many of the links are to demos of the commercial products that are available in the stores. This format allows you to "try before you buy."

Name:

Academy One

URL:

http://www.nptn.org/cyber.serv/AOneP/

Description of Site:

Academy One[R] is an international, online, educational resource for students, educators, parents, and administrators of grades kindergarten through 12. It is one of NPTN's (The National Public Telecomputing Network) three main interactive cybercasting services.

What to Do There:

Academy One coordinates several international education projects and simulations that promote cooperative learning and cooperation with teachers and students around the world. Some of these include the following: Legislation Simulation "How a Bill Becomes Law," Bird Migration Watch, Bridge Building Contest, Iditarod, Spotlight on People, Spotlight on Authors, and Spotlight on Student Authors.

Name:
Web66

URL:
http://web66.coled.umn.edu/

Description of Site:
Just as U.S. Highway Route 66 was a catalyst for Americana, we see the World Wide Web as a catalyst for integrating the Internet into K-12 school curricula. The Web66 project is designed to facilitate the introduction of this technology into K-12 schools. The goals of this project are the following:

1. To help K-12 educators learn how to set up their own Internet servers.
2. To link K-12 World Wide Web (WWW) servers, the educators, and the students at those schools.
3. To help K-12 educators find and use appropriate K-12 resources on the WWW.

What to Do There:
This site has all the technical information it takes to get your school up and running on the Internet's World Wide Web. It has information on networking, web authoring, as well as a nice directory of schools on the web. If you are ready to make your school a twenty-first century school, take a look here.

Name:

Dewey Web

URL:

http://ics.soe.umich.edu/

Description of Site:

You have reached the Dewey Web, an experiment in "global" education sponsored by ICS (Interactive Communications and Simulations) and the University of Michigan. The mission of Dewey Web is not only to provide information to students, but also to attempt to provide them a chance to contribute their own observations, findings, and reflections.

As time flashes by on the WWW, Dewey Web appears to be evolving into a sort of "clearinghouse" for experiments in electronic experiential education (or telecommunications-based education :-). Many projects using Dewey Web share staff and resources. This page consists of pointers to the real projects, where you can find out information about their staff, status, and participants.

What to Do There:

This site sports several resources for teachers including long and short-term projects and activities. One of the activities deals with an Arctic expedition that was undertaken in 1995. The students learn about the Arctic from the scientists' daily writing. It is arranged into several themes so that the teacher can customize the lessons to his/her curriculum.

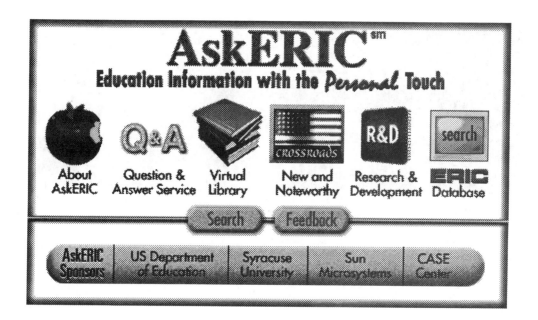

Name:

AskERIC

URL:

http://ericir.syr.edu/

Description of Site:

The Educational Resources Information Center (ERIC) is a federally funded, national information system that provides access to an extensive body of education-related literature. ERIC provides a variety of services and products at all education levels.

What to Do There:

Supported by the Educational Resources Information Center (ERIC), this site is the mother of educational resources and research. If you need information, they have it! Search for lesson plans, activities, or research on any educational topic you can think of.

Name:

EdWeb

URL:

http://edweb.gsn.org/

Description of Site:

The purpose of this hyperbook is to explore the worlds of educational reform and information technology. Using EdWeb, you can hunt down online educational resources around the world, learn about trends in education policy and information infrastructure development, examine success stories of computers in the classroom, and much, much more. EdWeb is a dynamic work-in-progress site, where numerous changes and additions occur on a regular basis.

What to Do There:

Named number one on the Net's Top Ten Educational Sites List, EdWeb has information that will help you with the basics of using the Internet in the classroom. Learn how to author your own web page, read discussions about child safety on the Internet, find out the role of the computer and the Internet in the classroom, and much more.

Name:

Yahoo's Education Search Engine

URL:

http://www.yahoo.com/Education/

Description of Site:

Yahoo is one of the most popular search engines on the Internet. (See Search Engines page 57.) It is divided into several categories, for example, business, entertainment, computers, and education. The above URL will take you directly to the Education category.

What to Do There:

To search the Yahoo Education index type in the name of the resource in which you are looking, click the Search only in Education radio button, and then click the Search button.

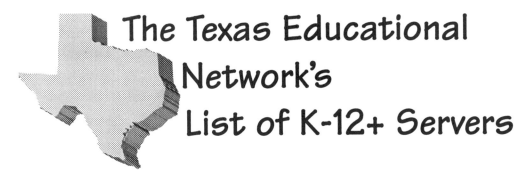

The Texas Educational Network's List of K-12+ Servers

Name:

The Texas Educational Network's List of K-12+ Servers

URL:

http://www.tenet.edu/education/main.html

Description of Site:

The Texas Educational Network (TENET) compiles a list of K–12 educational servers. Here you can find listings of schools that are on the Net, as well as other resources.

What to Do There:

Check out what other schools are doing on the Internet. Click U.S. K–12+ Servers by State, then choose the state from the map that you wish to search by clicking on it. This will bring you to a list of schools who support their own Internet pages. Several schools have taken this one step further and have added classroom web pages. See students' work, teachers' favorite sites, etc.

Educational **T**echnology **R**eview **C**enter

Name:

Educational Technology Network

URL:

http://www.edutechnet.com/

Description of Site:

The Educational Technology Network Web site is the result of a collaboration of professional educators and technologists committed to realizing the potential of technology in education.

What to Do There:

Looking for software that you know will work? Read the reviews of K-12 teachers before you invest your money. They will also help you find the resources you need to complete a unit. The "Best Practices" section is a must read for teachers or parents who wish to use technology in meaningful and productive ways.

Teacher's Edition Online

A Worldwide Forum for Teachers Sharing with Other Teachers

Name:

TeachNet.com

URL:

http://www.teachnet.com/

Description of Site:

TeachNet.com is an interactive teacher's magazine full of ideas that include the following: Lesson Plans, Classroom Decor, Getting Organized, Classroom Management, and Humor.

What to Do There:

Use the keypals section to set up electronic pen pals with students all over the country. Click Keypals in the menu, then click the grade level that you want. Read through the descriptions of classes and choose one to correspond with. Write or e-mail the teacher who is requesting keypals and describe your class and area. Next thing you know you will be corresponding on a regular basis.

Name:

CyberKids and CyberTeens

URL:

http://www.cyberkids.com/

Description of Site:

CyberKids' and CyberTeens' goal is to create and promote a worldwide youth community, as well as to give kids a voice and an interactive place to express their creativity. Young people all over the world make CyberKids a sharing, caring space. CyberKids is a place for kids' creativity to flourish while getting feedback from others; a space to read stories, to listen to kids' musical compositions, to view artwork, to meet keypals from all over the world.

What to Do There:

Have your students view the projects that have been published on the CyberKids or CyberTeen web sites. Then tell them that they can publish their work too. Have the students do a writing, multimedia, art, or music composition and then submit it to CyberKids or CyberTeens for publishing.

Midlink Magazine:
The Electronic Magazine for Kids in the Middle Grades

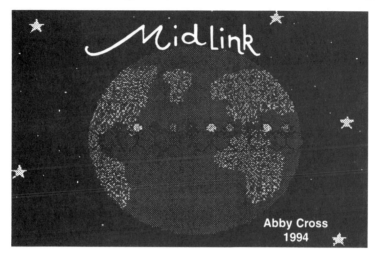

Name:

Midlink Magazine: The Electronic Magazine for Kids in the Middle Grades

URL:

http://longwood.cs.ucf.edu/~MidLink/

Description of Site:

MidLink Magazine, is an electronic magazine for kids in the middle grades—generally ages 10 to 15. Browse through the interactive space to enjoy art and writing that will link middle school kids all over the world. MidLink is published four times each year: fall, winter, spring, and summer. Every issue will have a new and exciting theme. You can participate just by logging in to their pages.

What to Do There:

Take part in Midlink's projects or start one of your own. Wondering about how social or environmental issues affect other people around the world? Decide as a class how you will experiment or collect data, then write up a procedure for others to follow. Submit this to Midlink following the instructions at their website, then wait for others to reply. Compare their analyses' to your own.

technology at work in east palo alto

Name:
Plugged In

URL:
http://www.pluggedin.org/

Description of Site:
Plugged In has helped to provide East Palo Alto, CA organizations and families with access to computer technology, serving as a nationally recognized model for connecting low-income communities with the information economy. Community members of all ages use state-of-the art computers to do online research, work on resumes, complete homework assignments, or participate in one of 30 classes offered in partnership with local agencies.

What to Do There:
If you are frustrated by the lack of technology in your area, plug in to this site. The information here under How Can You Do What We Do? can help you start a technology program in your school or community.

**U.S. DEPARTMENT OF EDUCATION
OFFICE OF EDUCATIONAL RESEARCH AND IMPROVEMENT
HELPING YOUR CHILD LEARN TO READ**

with activities for children from infancy through age 10

Name:

U.S. Department of Education—Office of Educational Research and Improvement Helping Your Child Learn to Read

URL:

http://www.ed.gov/pubs/parents/Reading/

Description of Site:

This site focuses primarily on what you can do to help children up to ten years of age. During these years you can lay the foundation for your child to become a lifelong reader. In the first section, you will find some basic information about reading to your child. This is followed by suggestions that guide you to read with your child and make this all-important time together enjoyable, stimulate your child's interest in reading and language, and learn about your child's school reading programs and find ways to help.

What to Do There:

This electronic book lays out a comprehensive method of helping parents help their children to read. Use the main menu as a reference of activities to do with your children from age 0-10. Some of the sections include the following: The Basics, Talking About Stories, Choosing Books, and Make a Book.

Machintosh Educator's Site

Name:

Macintosh Educator's Site

URL:

http://www.hampton-dumont.k12.ia.us/web/mac/default.html

Description of Site:

Maintained by the Hampton-Dumont Community School District of Hampton, Iowa, this site provides links to educational sites and technical assistance for Macintosh-using educators.

What to Do There:

If you are having trouble with your Mac or if you just want to find out how to do things more efficiently or creatively with it, click the Macintosh link and then choose an appropriate site for your question. There are also links to find free and low cost software for your Mac.

```
w w w . i l t . c o l u m b i a . e d u

   home   –   INDEX   –   search   –   about ILT  –
   projects  –  academic  –  internet  –  hot spots  –
```

Name:

Columbia University Institute for Learning Technologies: K-12 Resources

URL:

http://www.ilt.columbia.edu/k12/index.html

Description of Site:

Maintained by the Columbia University Institute for Learning Technologies: K–12 Resources, this site has several online resources and showcases for K–12 projects. The American History area is particularly good.

What to Do There:

If you teach American History, go to the American History Archive. Have your students view and comment on the work that has already been done by students at this site. Use the site to glean ideas and information for student projects that integrate technology into the curriculum.

Name:

Virtual Museums

URL:

http://www.icom.org/vlmp/

Description of Site:

Located at Oxford University, this is a well-maintained list of most museums throughout the world that have sites on the Internet. History museums are categorized for easy navigation.

What to Do There:

If you are having a hard time finding media, information, or resources on historic events, start here and browse the virtual museums around the world. This is also a good place to have students conduct a history scavenger hunt. Have them find digital pictures of famous paintings or text of famous documents and download them to their computer for use in projects.

KIDPROJ

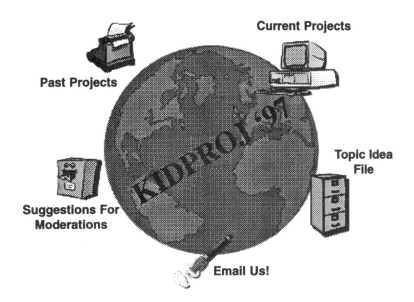

Current Projects

Past Projects

Topic Idea File

Suggestions For Moderations

Email Us!

Name:
KIDPROJ

URL:
http://www.kidlink.org/KIDPROJ/projects.html

Description of Site:
KIDPROJ is where teachers and youth group leaders from around the world organize activities and projects for students and other kids to participate in.

What to Do There:
One of the best things about the Internet is that it allows you to collaborate with people all over the world. KIDPROJ offers access to several projects that allow kids to collaborate internationally. Some past projects include the following: Desert & Desertification, Flags, Identify the Nut, Inventions, Kidlympics, Landmark Game, Math Penpals, Plate Tectonics, Readers' Corner, Robotics, SS Central America, Through Our Eyes, Wetlands, Whales, and Writers' Corner.

Name:

Think Quest

URL:

http://io.advanced.org/ThinkQuest/

Description of Site:

Ready to take the big plunge into the Internet? Think Quest is an annual contest that challenges students, ages 12 to 18, to use the Internet as a collaborative, interactive teaching and learning tool.

What to Do There:

Students from ages 12–18 collaborate to produce a web site project that communicates information to people around the world. Students will learn the Internet style of learning, then produce a project that teaches that style.

Name:

Internet Public Library

URL:

http://www.ipl.org/

Description of Site:

The Internet Public Library is the first public library of the Internet. They are committed to providing valuable services to that world. Their mission is the following: to provide library services to the Internet community, to learn and teach what librarians have to contribute in a digital environment, to promote librarianship and the importance of libraries, and to share interesting ideas and techniques with other librarians.

What to Do There:

The Internet public library provides several resources for research. The Internet Classroom section happens to be one of the best sections at this site. Have your students go there and take the interactive classes on how to use the Internet. This will help you teach them how to use this research tool with minimal effort and class time. Parents will also enjoy the lessons—they are good for any Internet beginner.

Consortium for School Networking

Name:

Consortium for School Networking

URL:

http://cosn.org/

Description of Site:

The CoSN server houses a wealth of material relating to school networking. A portion of this material will be reformatted and enriched with hypertext links. Other graphical material will also be put online through the present server.

What to Do There:

If you are looking for help getting your school networked, this is the place to start. They have information on networking, as well as schools' rights in this area. If you are looking for corporate or community sponsors, they can lead you in the right direction.

Name:

National PTA Online

URL:

http://www.pta.org/

Description of Site:

This site is dedicated to keeping parents and teachers abreast of the issues and initiatives that affect children. They also provide several resources from strengthening the home-school connection to talking with your children and teens about drugs and alcohol.

What to Do There:

Parents and educators will value the resources that the National PTA provides for them at this site. It is also a good site on which to read the organization's positions on various legislation that involves kids.

Name:

The Digital Education Network

URL:

http://www.actden.com/

Description of Site:

ACT is offering four DEN's to students seeking knowledge and fun. MathDEN presents a weekly set of competition-level questions for exceptional math students. GraphicsDEN shows students how to create cool computer graphics using an easy and affordable utility called Paint Shop Pro. NewsDEN presents local, national, and international current events in exciting new ways. InternetDEN offers online lessons that explain basic Internet tools and navigation.

What to Do There:

Have students log in and register with DEN. Each week they will be treated to problems in different curricular areas. They then complete the problems in the form of online tests. DEN tracks their progress, allowing them to see how well they are doing each week or cumulatively.

The Kid's Locker Room

Name:

The Kid's Locker Room

URL:

http://www.peg.apc.org/~balson/

Description of Site:

A kid's Internet site with an Australian twist. Explore over 5,000 Australian Web pages, links to 100s of Educational Webs, or use the resources of international search databases.

What to Do There:

If you are studying Australia, use the explore link to take you to over 5,000 Australian web sites. Have students compare the web culture in Australia against what they know of the United States. Collect pictures and other media about Australia. The educational links list is large and thorough.

Name:

Classroom Connect

URL:

http://www.classroom.net/

Description of Site:

Classroom Connect's home on the Internet is a site designed with the hope that it will become "homebase" to thousands of K–12 educators and students around the globe. The resources available here augment Classroom Connect's rapidly expanding line of product offerings which include newsletters, videos, books, seminars, training systems, software, and conferences.

What to Do There:

This site has one of the best sets of K–12 educational resources the Internet has to offer. Bookmark this site as a starting place to find curriculum sites that have been proven sound by educators. There is also a database of teachers that you can interact with through e-mail, as well as take part in online discussions.

Critical Evaluations Surveys

Name:

Critical Evaluations Surveys

URL:

http://www.capecod.net/schrockguide

Description of Site:

With the advent of the World Wide Web and the huge amount of information that is contained there, students need to be able to critically evaluate a Web page for authenticity, applicability, authorship, bias, and usability. The ability to critically evaluate information is an important skill in this information age. To help you get started with this process with your students, Kathy Schrock has designed a series of evaluation surveys, one each at the elementary, middle, and secondary school levels.

What to Do There:

Discuss what makes information valid and true. Ask students if everything that they find on the computer or Internet is always good information. Tell them that they must always decide if the information is valid. Pick an evaluation tool that matches the level of your children by clicking the hypertext. Print out the page and use it as a master to run off copies for your students. Assign your students each a separate web page to evaluate using the form.

Cool School Tools!

Name:

Cool School Tools!

URL:

http://www.bham.lib.al.us/cooltools/

Description of Site:

Cool School Tools! is an index to World Wide Web and other Internet resources for children and teenagers in grades K-12. Just like having a library in your living room, this site gives students links to reference materials and other resources catalogued loosely around the Dewey decimal system.

What to Do There:

When assigning homework to students who have computers at home, give them this site. They can use it to find information on specific topics or even use the built in tools like the dictionary, thesaurus, and quotations to enhance their writing.

Name:

Game Kids

URL:

http://www.gamekids.com/

Description of Site:

Game Kids is a gathering place for kids of all ages to learn and exchange non-computer games and activities. Each month, selected games and rhymes (traditional and contemporary), activities, and recipes will be selected from around the world for you to download, print out, and play. You are invited to submit your favorite games, stories, poetry, artwork, photographs, and recipes.

What to Do There:

Tired of kick ball and soccer? Use this site to find great physical education games that are kid tested and approved. Look through the teacher resource section for several links to related sites. You might even have your students write a description of a game to submit to Game Kids.

Smithsonian Education

Name:

Smithsonian—The Office of Elementary and Secondary Education

URL:

http://educate.si.edu

Description of Site:

The Office of Elementary and Secondary Education serves teachers and students across the country, as well as others interested in museum-related education. The office's programs, publications, and online networks inform teachers about Smithsonian educational resources and provide instructional approaches in art, language arts, science, and social studies.

What to Do There:

Surf here for several teacher resources and curriculum materials having to do with the Smithsonian. Many of these materials are online or available in book form for $5.00.

Education Listserv Mailing Lists

Name:

ERIC Education Listserv Mailing Lists

URL:

gopher://ericir.syr.edu:70/11/Listservs

Description of Site:

An archived list of Education Listserv mailing lists on the Internet and the messages that were posted to them.

What to Do There:

Browse through the Listservs' mail messages to get an idea what types of subjects each covers. Then join the lists that you think might be helpful. (See subscribing to listservs on pages 29-32.) Do not subscribe to too many at a time or else you will be inundated with mail.

Over 20,000 personalities!
Over 1,500 home videos!

Name:

Biography

URL:

http://www.biography.com

Description of Site:

The Biography.com database puts over 20,000 of the greatest lives, past and present, at your fingertips. Enter a name in the "Search" box provided to discover who they were, what they did and why. When you get to the site you are greeted by a list of biographies of famous people who were born on that day.

What to Do There:

Print out and read a biography a day. Have your students look up biographies of famous people that were born on their birthdays. Use the site to teach biographies and then have students write their own biography.

Name:

Columbia Education Center's Mini Lessons

URL:

http://youth.net/cec/cec.html

Description of Site:

This group of lesson plans came from the Columbia Education Center's Summer Workshops. They were done by a consortium of teachers from 14 states dedicated to improving the quality of education in the rural, western, United States, particularly the quality of math and science education.

What to Do There:

This is a great place to get lesson plans. The site is divided into subject areas and then by grade level: Elementary School, Intermediate School, and High School. Just decide what subject area and grade level you wish and click that hypertext link. A list of hypertext titles and lesson plans with suggested grade levels will be displayed. Click any in which you are interested and the lesson plan will be displayed. If you like it, choose Print in your browser's menu. Choose the Back button to take you back up a level.

MetaCrawler

Name:

MetaCrawler

URL:

http://www.metacrawler.com/

Description of Site:

The problem with finding information on the Internet is just that, finding information on the Internet. Search engines are great, but they rely on people registering sites with them. Some search engines might have one sight that another does not have. MetaCrawler is a search engine of search engines. It checks for the information you want in several search engines and returns the results. This method is much less time consuming.

What to Do There:

Just like other search engines, input the key words that you are searching for. Make sure you narrow down the search parameters as much as possible by choosing an area like "science education" as opposed to just "education" to search.

Web Sites And Resources For Teachers

Name:

Web Sites and Resources for Teachers

URL:

http://www.csun.edu/~vceed009

Description of Site:

Dr. Vicki F. Sharp and Dr. Richard M. Sharp are Professors of Elementary Education at California State University, Northridge. They have collected sites and resources from the Internet for teachers to use in their classrooms. There is also a special category for children called "Just for Kids". These sites are entertaining, useful, informative, and fun. They range from lesson plans, to creative classroom projects, to interactive activities, to visits to museums, to trips around the U.S.A. and other countries. They are organized in eight categories.

What to Do There:

This is a fantastic collection of resources that the authors update very regularly. The site is divided by subject area, then by grade level, and finally by subtopic. For example, if you were looking for online literature you would click the language arts icon which would take you to the language arts page. From there you can click the literature hypertext or scroll through the sheet until you find what you are looking for. Remember, the Back button on your browser will always take you back to the last place you were. Keep clicking back to take you step-by-step back through your sequence of moves.

Name:

LiveText Educational Resources

URL:

http://www.ilt.columbia.edu/k12/livetext/

Description of Site:

LiveText is a comprehensive, annotated, structured index to online resources relating to network technologies and their use in K–12 schools. LiveText is being developed by the Institute for Learning Technologies at Teachers College, Columbia University to support teachers and administrators in integrating technology into the curriculum and classroom.

What to Do There:

Another great search engine based solely on integrating technology into education. Sites and resources are grouped several ways so that users can make connections of the resources to any part of the curriculum that the resource supports. When you arrive at the site for the first time read the Navigation Guide and Beginner's Guide. These can be reached by clicking the hypertext of the same name.

Name:

Technology and Learning Online

URL:

http://www.techlearning.com

Description of Site:

Technology and Learning Online is brought to you by the publishers of Technology & Learning magazine, the leading publication for technology-using educators. This companion site offers an overview of the magazine, as well as some Internet related items not found in the publication.

What to Do There:

Looking for software, but don't know what to buy? Tired of wasting your money on software that you don't use? Surf to this site to read reviews of software products. To get there, click the Software Reviews icon, then choose the subject area you wish by clicking the box to the left of the subject. Finally click Search and you will be given a list of articles that compare software in that area.

Search Database of Software Reviews Form

Select the criteria that meet your interests and then click the Search button below.

(Search) (Clear)

Select one or more subjects:
(Your search will include all subjects if you do not select a subject.)

☐ Reading/Language Arts	☐ Foreign Language/ESL
☒ Math	☐ Reference Tools
☐ Science	☐ Especially for Special Education
☐ Social Studies	☐ Guidance/Life Skills
☐ Early Childhood/Readiness	☐ Test Preparation/Study Skills
☐ Music/Art Appreciation & History	☐ Computer Literacy/Programming/Keyboarding
☐ Creativity/Multimedia Tools	☐ School Management (gradebooks, file utilities, etc.)
☐ Word Processing/Desktop Publishing	☐ Online and Internet
☐ Problem Solving/Thinking Skills	

Name:

Core Knowledge Lesson Plans and Units

URL:

http://www.trinity.edu/departments/education/core/newplans.htm

Description of Site:

This site is a depository of lesson plans and units, created by teachers throughout the country using the Core Knowledge Sequence. Please look through them and use them in your own classrooms.

What to Do There:

Click the hypertext that corresponds to the subject in which you are interested. Your web browser will display a listing of all the lesson and unit plans for that subject arranged by grade level. Click the hypertext title to review the lesson and print if you like it.

Name:

CyberSurfari

URL:

http://www.spa.org/cybersurfari/

Description of Site:

The Software Publishers Association invites you to join the one-month Internet adventure that embarks every October from the treasure map at CyberSurfari headquarters. The map reveals ten CyberStations that hold the clues needed to find treasure located at each of 100 CyberSurfari outposts scattered across the uncharted wilderness of cyberspace.

What to Do There:

A perfect way for students to learn how to navigate the WWW and maybe even win something. Have students sign up at this site then follow the directions for the date and time to join in on this Internet scavenger hunt.

Name:
23 Peaks Expedition

URL:
http://www.23peaks.com

Description of Site:
Students take part in an expedition of explorers who seek to climb the highest peaks in the Western hemisphere. Read journal entries and look at daily photographs of the expedition.

What to Do There:
As the explorers report back to base (your home or class), you use the activities and information to research the areas which they visit. You can even communicate through e-mail or look at the FAQ file. You become a vital part of the expedition. Go directly to the Info area to find out more about this adventure.

The University of Texas, Austin
College of Education
Dept. of Curriculum and Instruction
Area of Instructional Technology

Name:

Electronic Emissary

URL:

http://www.tapr.org/emissary/

Description of Site:

The Electronic Emissary Project is a new type of Internet-based interpersonal resource that has been online since February of 1993. It is based at the University of Texas at Austin, in the College of Education. The Emissary is a "matching service" that helps teachers with access to the Internet locate other Internet account-holders who are experts in different disciplines, for purposes of setting up curriculum-based, electronic exchanges among the teachers, their students, and the experts. In this way, the interaction that occurs among teachers and students face-to-face in the classroom is supplemented and extended by exchanges that occur among teachers, students, and SME's asynchronously via electronic mail.

What to Do There:

Imagine being able to exchange information and get advice from scientists and other experts on projects which your students are working on. The Electronic Emissary helps you set this up while not burdening experts with tons of e-mail. To check this out, click the hypertext "The Project".

Name:

Global SchoolNet

URL:

http://www.gsn.org

Description of Site:

Global SchoolNet is a storehouse of hundreds of Internet resources for teachers.

What to Do There:

This award winning site is in the author's opinion one of the best the Web has to offer for teaching and learning. Check out the "Projects" link for information on several ongoing collaborative projects in which you can connect your students and classrooms with others all over the world. Create your own project or just join in on one that has already been developed. It is exciting, authentic learning and fun at the same time.

ACEKids

Name:

ACEKids

URL:

http://www.acekids.com

Description of Site:

ACEKids is a certified kid safe site that offers several educational, as well as entertainment, activities for kids.

What to Do There:

Another good site for students to learn how to navigate through the World Wide Web. Visit the site yourself and find several links, activities, and media that you would like for your students to see or find. Write up a scavenger hunt sheet full of those items that you want them to collect or find. Then turn them loose (always with supervision) and have them find the items. Award them points for each item found.

****Reminder:** Even though this site is rated kid safe, there are always ways out of an area and into one that might not be as appropriate. Use one of the security programs listed on page 13 and always supervise children when using the Internet.

Name:
Teacher Created Materials

URL:
http://www.teachercreated.com

Description of Site:
Teacher Created Materials, Inc. publishes teacher made, tested, and approved materials (including this book). This site offers free lesson plans and other teacher resources. Check out the technology materials they offer.

What to Do There:
I know, a shameless plug for Teacher Created Materials. But the materials are the best on the market because teachers like you create them. Send them an e-mail if you have materials that you would like published. Proposals should include an outline of the unit and two to three sample pages. You never know, you might be published and get paid for something that you already do in the classroom.

Name:

The Electronic Zoo

URL:

http://netvet.wustl.edu/history.htm

Description of Site:

The Electronic Zoo is a collection of animal information from all over the Internet.

What to Do There:

Have students use this site to find out information about any animal that they can think of. Teach classification by having each student search through the Animal database. Then have each student think of a specific animal, by clicking the family he/she thinks that the animal belongs to. Narrow the families down until he/she has found the specific animal he/she was thinking of. Then read the information about the animal to learn more.

Name:

The Exploratorium Exploranet

URL:

http://www.exploratorium.edu/

Description of Site:

This site was developed as a guide for the museum in San Francisco, but soon branched out to include some digital representations of the experiments that are included in the actual museum.

What to Do There:

Click the menu item Digital Library of Exhibits and explore some of the experiments. The experiments on visual acuity are amazing. Try Shimmer—Your eye movements make this design seem to shimmer. Fading Dot—If you stare at this dot for a few moments it disappears.

JASON VIII: Journey From the Center of the Earth

Name:

The JASON Project

URL:

http://www.jasonproject.org

Description of Site:

The JASON Project brings the thrill of exploration and discovery live to students around the world as they participate in amazing electronic field trips.

What to Do There:

The JASON Project is an exciting electronic field trip in which students interact with and actually dictate the course that scientists will take.

There are several ways to become involved in the year-round JASON Project. The highest level of involvement is participation in the activities of a Primary Interactive Network Site (PINS). This type of involvement allows interactive access to the scientists but because of network considerations, is out of the reach of most schools. I recommend receiving educational television broadcasts via the JASON Classroom Network, and gaining access to JASON Project information and activities on the Internet. There are several lesson plans and activities that make this project one of the best on the Internet.

Name:

StarChild

URL:

http://starchild.gsfc.nasa.gov/docs/StarChild/StarChild.html/

Description of Site:

The StarChild site is a service of the High Energy Astrophysics Science Archive
Research Center (HEASARC), within the Laboratory for High Energy
Astrophysics (LHEA) at NASA. It is a depository of several images that have
been collected by NASA covering the following subjects: Astronomy, The Earth,
Galaxies, The Moon, Planets, Space, Stars, The Sun, and The Universe.

What to Do There:

This is an excellent site to gather digital pictures and information for kids' reports
and presentations. To copy a picture in most web browsers just place the cursor
on the picture that you want, then hold down the mouse button. A menu of
choices will appear. Choose Save As, then give the picture a name. Click Save
after you have navigated to the folder or directory that you wish to place the
pictures in. Now the picture will be available for placement in a word processing
document or presentation program.

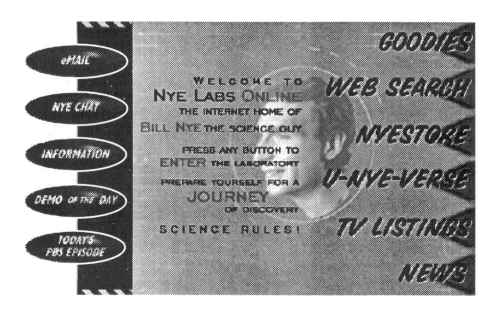

Name:

Nye Labs Online

URL:

http://nyelabs.kcts.org/

Description of Site:

Nye Labs Online is a companion site for the popular PBS television show "Bill Nye, The Science Guy." Among some of the things to do at the site are the following: e-mail Bill Nye, view video clips of the show, get instructions on how to do the experiments that were done in an episode, and find out about episodes that are airing today.

What to Do There:

Watch an episode in class or at home, then go to the web site and read the follow-up activity in "Demo of the Day." This section will summarize the basic concepts discussed in the show and give an experiment to do as a follow-up extension activity. After you are finished, send an e-mail to Bill Nye or any of the people who work on the show by clicking the e-mail button.

Name:

The Franklin Institute Science Museum

URL:

http://sln.fi.edu/

Description of Site:

The Franklin Institute Science Museum brings the exhibits, resources, and fun of a museum visit right to your desktop.

What to Do There:

Tour online exhibits, educational hotlists, and the publications library where you will find other science news, activities, and resources. Use these units of study to support your science curriculum.

U.S. DEPARTMENT OF EDUCATION

OFFICE OF EDUCATIONAL RESEARCH AND IMPROVEMENT

PROGRAMS FOR THE IMPROVEMENT OF PRACTICE

HELPING YOUR CHILD LEARN SCIENCE

Name:

Helping Your Child Learn Science

URL:

http://www.ed.gov/pubs/parents/Science/index.html

Description of Site:

This site suggests ways you can interest your children from about three to ten years of age in science. It includes the following: Some basic information about science; A sampling of activities for children to do—some alone, some with supervision—in both the home and the community; An Appendix with practical tips on how to encourage schools to develop good science programs; a brief description of nine scientific concepts; and a list of recommended science books and magazines.

What to Do There:

Read the information in The Basics section about how to teach science, then try one of the over 30 activities that are written for children ages three through ten.

Name:
Volcano World

URL:
http://volcano.und.nodak.edu/

Description of Site:
Volcanoes are one of the most dramatic phenomena in nature, attracting millions of visitors each year to U.S. national parks, and fascinating millions more children in school science courses. Volcano World greatly enriches the learning experiences of these children by delivering high quality remote sensing images, other data, and interactive experiments that add depth, variety, and currency to existing volcano information sources.

What to Do There:
Go through the kid's door by clicking the Kid's Door hypertext link. Once there, view Kids' Volcano Art, take the Kid Quiz, go on Virtual Field Trips, e-mail questions for real volcanists in the Kid's Door Mail and they will post the answers for all to see, and much more.

Views of the Solar System by Calvin J. Hamilton

Views of the Solar System
by Calvin J. Hamilton

Name:

Views of the Solar System

URL:

http://bang.lanl.gov/solarsys/

Description of Site:

Views of the Solar System has been created as an educational tour of the solar system. It contains images and information about the Sun, planets, moons, asteroids, comets, and meteoroids found within the solar system. It contains over 220 pages of information, over 950 high-resolution images and animations, and over 880 megabytes of data. The image processing for many of the images were done by the author Calvin J. Hamilton.

What to Do There:

Take a virtual field trip of the solar system by clicking the planet that you want to visit. Once you have arrived at a planet, you will be greeted with information and several pictures. Collect the information for research reports by printing or copying and pasting the text. Most web browsers allow you to save the pictures by simply holding down on the mouse button while the cursor is over the picture. Then select Save As from the FILE menu, give the picture a name, and save it in an appropriate place. Later you can use the pictures in your reports or presentations, but make sure you give the author credit by footnoting the picture or quote. Have students take part in a scavenger hunt of the solar system by compiling a list of properties that are unique to a planet. Students would then search for the planet that has those properties.

Name:

The Ontario Science Centre

URL:

http://www.osc.on.ca/

Description of Site:

The Ontario Science Centre web site gives you a virtual tour of their exhibits, online science experiments at the Interactive Zone, a list of Web Connections, and several educational programs that have been tested by teachers.

What to Do There:

Go to the Interactive Zone and try the experiments. You will need to download the Shockwave Plug in for your web browser at http://www.macromedia.com/shockwave/ in order to do the experiments, but it is worth the time. Kids and parents will be amazed by the color mixing experiments.

Name:

You Can with Beakman and Jax

URL:

http://www.beakman.com

Description of Site:

This is a companion site to the popular TV show "Beakman's World." You Can has answers to your questions and interactive science demos. It also has links to other terrific World Wide Web sites. Using You Can, you can find out what is coming up in future editions of You Can with Beakman & Jax on the TV show "Beakman's World." Many of the images are really buttons you can click to see what happens. Some of the buttons are secret, so you will have to explore for yourself.

What to Do There:

Students always have questions about their world. Brainstorm a list of questions like, "Why is the sky blue?" or "Why is a diamond so hard?" Then follow the Answers to Your Questions link to find out the why's. If they don't have an answer to your question, e-mail it to them and check back later. It will probably be answered.

Name:

Whales: A Thematic Unit

URL:

http://curry.edschool.virginia.edu:80/~kpj5e/Whales/

Description of Site:

The Whales home page provides a thematic unit for cooperative learning across an integrated curriculum, which is an interactive resource for teachers, students, and parents.

What to Do There:

This unit has been compiled by several teachers and also anyone who reviews it and wants to make additions or comments. Use the entire set of activities and resources or just what you want. Some of the activities are based upon links to other sites, while others stand on their own. Sections of the unit include the following: Teacher Resources, Student Activities, Whale Projects, and Internet Resources.

Name:

Discovery Channel School

URL:

http://school.discovery.com/

Description of Site:

Discovery Channel Online is full of interactive stories about science, nature, history, people, and more. Educators will love the School section.

What to Do There:

The Discovery Channel allows educators to tape shows for use in their classrooms. Even better, they help you find appropriate programming to match your curriculum, give you follow-up activities and lesson plans, and even tell you how to set your VCR to tape the program. Use the Resource Finder to narrow your search by clicking the button that corresponds to your grade level or curriculum need. You will then see a list of programs that match your search. Choose a program and you will get all the resources that go with it.

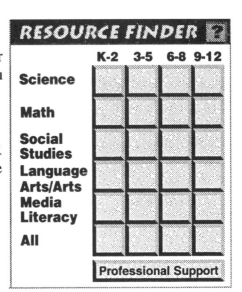

Name:
Students for the Exploration and Development of Space

URL:
http://www.seds.org/

Description of Site:
Students for the Exploration and Development of Space (SEDS) is an independent, student-based organization which promotes the exploration and development of space. SEDS pursues this mission by educating people about the benefits of space, supporting a network of interested students, providing an opportunity for members to develop their leadership skills, and inspiring people through their involvement in space-related projects. SEDS believes in a space-faring civilization and that focusing the enthusiasm of young people is the key to our future in space.

What to Do There:
Have students think about the colonization of the moon or other planets. Then have them explore the Visions of the Future and Space Station links to get information about the topic. Then have them develop their own moon or planet community by drawing plans and writing a story about the colony. Once they are finished have your students log-in to the chat site by clicking the Chat link. Make sure you check the schedule of chat times first. Have them discuss their plans with other students.

WELCOME TO
ENC Online

Choose your connection to
explore this site for the best
selection of K-12 mathematics and
science resources on the Internet!

Eisenhower National
C l e a r i n g h o u s e

for frames-capable browsers
⮕ **HIGH TECH**

for earlier browsers
⮕ **LOW TECH**

Name:

Eisenhower National Clearinghouse (ENC)

URL:

http://www.enc.org/

Description of Site:

The Eisenhower National Clearinghouse (ENC) is a nationally recognized
information source for K–12 mathematics and science teachers.

What to Do There:

This site houses tons of information on science and math education. Browse
through the lesson plans section or look at the collaborative projects that are
linked to these pages.

Tellecollaborative Learning Around the World

Name:

Telecollaborative Learning Around the World

URL:

http://www1.minn.net:80/~schubert/NickNacks.html

Description of Site:

NickNacks' primary goal is to encourage collaborations among educators and students around the world. Whether you want to participate in a lesson or start your own, there is information here to help you. Together we can build a better place to live, grow, and learn.

What to Do There:

Want to take part in collaborative lessons with classes all over the world? Here is a great place to start. If you don't find a project you like, make up your own. They will help you with starting your own project, as well as help you get other classes to participate.

Name:
Integrating the Internet

URL:
http://seamonkey.ed.asu.edu/~hixson/index/

Description of Site:
Lots of people are talking about this topic, but there are relatively few places to go to find out about it. Look here to find primary resources, projects, a weekly newsletter, units of study, and a tutorial to help you plan projects and classroom home pages.

What to Do There:
This site has several activities in the science area. Ready to make the jump to producing your own pages on the Web? Susan Hixson has given you everything you need to do it here—from directions on design and producing, to how you get web space, to placing your document.

Welcome to the Virtual Earthquake

Name:

Virtual Earthquake

URL:

http://vflylab.calstatela.edu/edesktop/VirtApps/VirtualEarthQuake/VQuakeIntro.html

Description of Site:

Virtual Earthquake is an interactive computer program designed to introduce you to the concepts of how an earthquake epicenter is located and how the Richter magnitude of an earthquake is determined. The Virtual Earthquake computer program is running on a World Wide Web Server at California State University at Los Angeles. You can interact with Virtual Earthquake through your Web browser, provided your browser supports "forms".

What to Do There:

This is a great lesson on integrating math and science. Print out the background information on the first page of this site. Then study it closely with your students. After this is done, send students to the computer to explore the site. Have them chose an area for the simulated earthquake and then read the seismographs. They determine the epicenter with the information provided.

Name:

Science On-line Toolkit

URL:

http://cse.ssl.berkeley.edu/

Description of Site:

Visitors to this site will find ready-made classroom activities developed by educators, as well as images, interactive tools, text, and other resources to help you build your own Internet-based classroom activities.

What to Do There:

Great place to find lesson plans and activities in any of the disciplines of science.

Name:

Cloud Catalog

URL:

http://covis.atmos.uiuc.edu/guide/clouds/html/cloud.home.html

Description of Site:

We see clouds almost every day. To observe them and to identify them, all you need is your eyes. A cloud is comprised of visible ice crystals and/or water droplets suspended in air. Clouds can be big or little, thick or thin, existing in a seemingly endless array of shapes and sizes. The purpose of these pages is to introduce how clouds develop and their different families.

What to Do There:

Start by using the site to learn about different cloud types. The site is divided into short chapters about the different cloud types. Then use the activities in the Suggested Classroom Activities section. If you want to do reports or stories about the clouds, use the photographs on the pages in a word processor or paint program. Make sure that you give the site credit.

Name:

Science Daily

URL:

http://www.sciencedaily.com

Description of Site:

Every day, Science Daily brings you the latest stories about discoveries in science, technology, and medicine gathered from the leading science news sites on the Internet. Science Daily also provides links to news releases from the world's leading universities and research centers. Readers can subscribe to a free weekly e-mail update that summarizes the news of the past week.

What to Do There:

Super place for science based current events. Have students find an article relating to something that is being studied in class, then have them report to the class on that subject.

Name:
The Froggy Page

URL:
http://www.cs.yale.edu/HTML/YALE/CS/HyPlans/loosemore-sandra/froggy.html

Description of Site:
If it has to do with frogs, it is here including digital frog pictures, digital frog sounds, frog literature, frog science, and all kinds of other froggy stuff.

What to Do There:
If you are doing an integrated unit on animals or you just like frogs, this site is a gold mine. Read your class the frog literature, take part in a virtual frog dissection, and even find out some great physical education activities based on, you guessed it, leap frog.

Name:

The Weather Channel

URL:

http://www.weather.com

Description of Site:

This site is a repository of the most up to date satellite pictures and movies, as well as other weather information on the web. Images are updated constantly, but to see the most recent ones you will have to click Reload on your browser utility.

What to Do There:

Copy several images over a set amount of time. Try to copy these images at equal intervals. Using a slide show presentation program like *Kid Pix Studio*, *HyperStudio*, *ClarisWorks* or *MicroSoft Works,* have your students make a slide show of the images. Tell them to observe the movement of the weather systems and make generalizations.

Name:

Science Friday Kids Connection

URL:

http://www.npr.org/programs/sfkids

Description of Site:

This site is intended to be a companion to National Public Radio's Science
Friday broadcast. However, using the Real Audio Plug In
(http://www.realaudio.com) you can hear the broadcast via your computer. The
site includes activities to use in class, as well as a section that allows you to ask
questions of scientists.

What to Do There:

Check the Previous Weeks' broadcasts and curricula to see if any match your
units of study. Listen to the broadcasts over the Internet using the Real Audio
Player listed above and do the follow-up activities with your students. E-mail
messages to the scientists to clear up questions that you may have.

Name:

Virtual Science and Mathematics Fair

URL:

http://134.121.112.29/fair_95/gym/index.html

Description of Site:

This is just like the science fairs we have at school, but in cyberspace, where there is a potential audience of millions. Enter your science projects in the form of a paper. The results and methods are judged and all are displayed at the web site.

What to Do There:

If your students already take part in a science fair, simply submit a written summary of their experiment to this site. It will be published on the Internet and judged against other students in the same grade level.

Name:

The Science Learning Network

URL:

http://www.sln.org/

Description of Site:

The Science Learning Network (SLN) is an online community of educators, students, schools, science museums, and other institutions demonstrating a new model for inquiry science education.

What to Do There:

Learn how to conduct inquiry science lessons in your classroom, then use the unit and lesson plan resources in your classroom. Collaborate with other teachers by signing up in the Collaborate and Share Ideas section of the site.

Minnesota Department of Transportation's
Aeronautics Server

Name:

Aeronautical Information Server

URL:

http://www.dot.state.mn.us/aeronautics/mdot.html

Description of Site:

Supported by the Minnesota Department of Transportation, this site includes educational materials for teachers and students interested in aviation.

What to Do There:

Use this site as part of a unit on flight for careers. Use the educational resources including lesson plans and work sheets, enter the art contest, or find out what it takes to become a pilot.

Name:

The Bear Den

URL:

http://www2.portage.net/~dmiddlet/bears/index.html

Description of Site:

This web site is dedicated to the following goals: contributing to a comprehensive understanding of all members of the ursidae (bear) family, allowing visitors to share in a visual and written celebration of the wonder we experience in the presence of bears, and supporting the successful cohabitation of bears and humans upon the earth.

What to Do There:

This site contains everything that you ever wanted to know about bears but were afraid to ask—this site is a conglomeration of information, stories, and media about these furry creatures. Use this site when you are studying omnivores, animal classification, or just plain ol' bears. The photos are fantastic for reports or other writings.

Name:

Cells alive!

URL:

http://www.cellsalive.com/

Description of Site:

This web site is dedicated to the study of cellular life. It is full of animations showing several different types of cells in motion.

What to Do There:

This site is too cool! Use this site to teach students all about life at the cellular level. Each subject uses video clips and animations to illustrate things like how bacteria divide, how antibodies are formed, how the HIV virus travels from cell to cell, as well as much more. Use the Web site live as a visual aide or download the animations to use offline. You will need *Netscape 2.0* or *Internet Explorer 3.0* or higher to view the animations.

Name:

SeaWorld/Busch Gardens Animal Information Database

URL:

http://www.seaworld.org/

Description of Site:

In addition to animal information resources, SeaWorld Busch Gardens provides teachers visiting this site with several activities that they can do in class. Take the animal quizzes and collect pictures and video media for projects.

What to Do There:

Explore this site for information and resources that have to do with animals. If students are collecting data about animals, try the hypertext link for Animal Bytes (fast facts about animals). These are organized in outline fashion. This is good in that students can write their reports in their own words using accurate facts.

Science and Mathematics

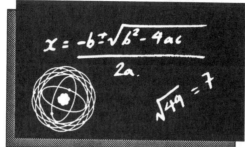

Education Resources

Name:

SciEd: Science and Mathematics Education Resources

URL:

http://www-hpcc.astro.washington.edu/scied/science.html

Description of Site:

Supported by the University of Washington, this site is a directory of science and mathematics resources on the Internet. Resources are grouped into the following categories: Astronomy and Space Science, Physics, Chemistry, Earth Sciences, Biological Sciences, Mathematics, Multiple Disciplines, Paleontology, Anthropology/Archeology, Science Museums and Exhibits, History of Science, Doing Science, Ethics in Science, Skepticism and Pseudoscience, Science Reference Shelf, Suppliers of Equipment and Software, and Science Education Organizations.

What to Do There:

If you are searching for science or math resources click the hypertext for the category in which you are searching. Read the overviews and link to a site by clicking its name.

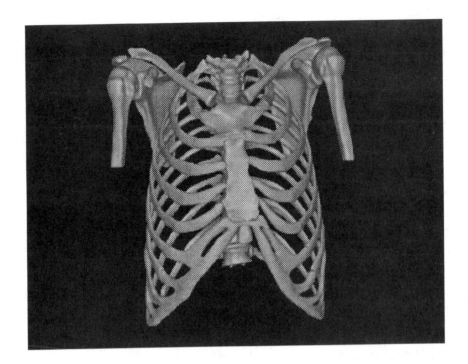

Name:

Virtual Anatomy Image Browser

URL:

http://www.vis.colostate.edu/cgi-bin/gva/gvaview

Description of Site:

Do not just show your students pictures of body systems from books. At this site you can decide what structures you want to look at and then view them from any angle.

What to Do There:

Discuss any of the organ systems that are covered at the site using a computer that is connected to this site as a visual aide. Rotate images to see anything that your students are interested in. Have your students collect media from this site for use in presentations and/or reports. Make sure to name Colorado State University as your source when using the images.

Name:

The International Food Information Council for Educators

URL:

http://ificinfo.health.org/info-ed.htm

Description of Site:

The IFIC provides teachers with several lesson and unit plans that teach students to make good food choices. Some of the lesson plans that they offer are Play it Safe: Food Safety Educational Curriculum (grades 4-6), and Kids Make the Nutritional Grade (grades 6-9).

What to Do There:

Read the information and print the sample lessons to use in class. You can order the printed materials at a nominal fee.

Name:

Benny Goodsport

URL:

http://www.bennygoodsport.com

Description of Site:

Benny and colorful Goodsport Gang characters teach kids that healthy living and fitness is fun! This interactive site features lots to see and do including games, sports, stories, and other fun activities.

What to Do There:

- have your students submit stories
- print crossword puzzles and other activities to use in the classroom or at home
- learn new outdoor and indoor games that promote a healthy lifestyle
- learn about nutrition

Name:

Math Magic

URL:

http://forum.swarthmore.edu/mathmagic/

Description of Site:

Math Magic is a K–12 telecommunications project developed in El Paso, Texas. It provides strong motivation for students to use computer technology while increasing problem-solving strategies and communications skills. Math Magic posts challenges in each of four categories (K–3, 4–6, 7–9, and 10–12) to trigger each registered team to pair up with another team and engage in a problem-solving dialog. When an agreement has been reached, one solution is posted for every pair.

What to Do There:

Sign up for an adventure using Math. You will be given a partner team at your grade level somewhere in the world. Each week you get a problem to solve. After working/communicating with your partner team via e-mail to solve the problem, post your answer to see if you are right. Try a few of the challenges without signing up to see if you like it. A donation of $12.00 is requested for every four-student team per year.

Name:

Mega Math

URL:

http://www.c3.lanl.gov/mega-math/welcome.html

Description of Site:

The Mega Math project is intended to bring unusual and important mathematical ideas to elementary school classrooms so that young people and their teachers can think about them together.

What to Do There:

This site lets elementary age kids contemplate more advanced mathematical concepts at their level. Concepts like infinity are broken down in activities that make students contemplate the concept. Use the activity menu shown to explore all aspects of the activities.

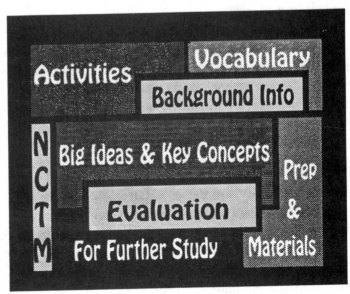

STEVE'S DUMP THE MATH FORUM INTERNET RESOURCE COLLECTION
SEARCHABLE ANNOTATED

Name:

The Math Forum: Steve's Dump

URL:

http://forum.swarthmore.edu/~steve/index.html

Description of Site:

There is an overwhelming amount of "stuff" on the Internet and a high percentage of it has little substance, although this is rapidly changing. Part of our task, as we see it, is to make it easy for mathematicians and math teachers to find the resources available for their purposes. This site will help you find what you are looking for.

What to Do There:

Use several different curriculum search engines to find what you are looking for. Just click the link named a Quick Search and input what you are looking for in the box, then click Search. A list will be generated that applies to the word that you inputted. For example, when the word fractions was entered, the search brought back over 75 links to documents and sites that contained the word.

Find entries containing (put spaces between keywords):

[   ]

[Search] [Reset]

 # Puzzle Archive

Name:

The Puzzle Archive

URL:

http://alabanza.com/kabacoff/Inter-Links/puzzles.html

Description of Site:

This site is an archive of puzzles and brain teasers from the newsgroup rec.puzzles and are categorized by subject. Both the puzzles and their solutions are given.

What to Do There:

Need extra activities for starters at the beginning of Math class? Maybe you just need to keep those more mathematically inclined kids challenged when working with another group. This site has literally hundreds of puzzles and brain teasers at several different levels.

Name:

Ask Dr. Math

URL:

http://forum.swarthmore.edu/dr.math/

Description of Site:

This site is the place to go when you want answers. If you or your students have questions about a math problem, Dr. Math will help you figure it out.

What to Do There:

Submit your K–12 math question by sending e-mail to dr.math@forum.swarthmore.edu. Tell them what you know about your problem and where you are stuck. Dr. Math will reply to you via e-mail.

Elementary Problem of the Week

Name:
Elementary Problem of the Week

URL:
http://forum.swarthmore.edu/sum95/ruth/elem.pow.html

Description of Site:
High school students pose challenging problems for elementary students
each week.

What to Do There:
One of hundreds of grass roots mathematics projects out there that will help you
bring spice to your math program. Log on each week and print out the problem
of the week. After your students have solved the problem, post the answer in
their posting section. You will be rewarded for attempting whether you are right
or not.

Name:

The Explorer

URL:

http://unite.ukans.edu/

Description of Site:

The Explorer is a collection of educational resources (e.g., instructional software, lab activities, lesson plans, etc.) for K–12 mathematics and science education. You may browse through mathematics and science curricula or conduct searches that focus on specific interests.

What to Do There:

Browse the hundreds of free math and science units and lesson plans. They are currently available for downloading in *ClarisWorks* and *Adobe Acrobat* format. If you don't have *ClarisWorks*, download the *Adobe Acrobat* reader right at this site. You will find it at http://www.adobe.com/acrobat/. These files are readable by Mac, Windows, and DOS computers.

Name:

The Math Forum

URL:

http://forum.swarthmore.edu/

Description of Site:

There are many good sites. That is the excitement and the challenge of the Internet. Our goal is to build a community that can be a center for teachers, students, researchers, parents, educators, citizens at all levels who have an interest in mathematics education.

What to Do There:

Another great place to search for math resources. Check out the Teacher's Place. This area is full of curriculum and content based on math. If you want to start your own project, this is another great place to begin.

History of Mathematics

Name:

The History of Mathematics

URL:

http://aleph0.clarku.edu/~djoyce/mathhist/mathhist.html

Description of Site:

This site is just what it says, The History of Mathematics. Dr. David Joyce has compiled information about famous mathematicians and their theories and discoveries.

What to Do There:

Use the menu below to navigate through the site. Try clicking Timelines and Chronology to see how each mathematician built on, proved, and disproved theories of earlier mathematicians.

Home	Web	Subjects	Regions	Books
Timelines	Chronology	File Index	Mall	

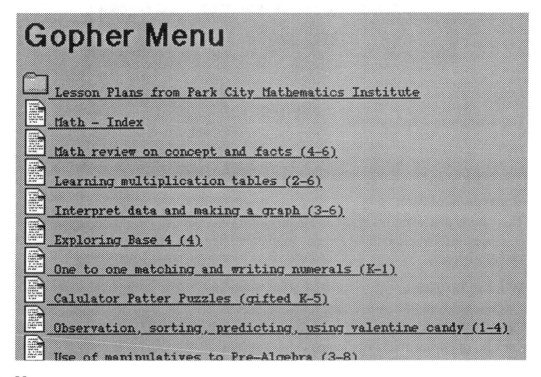

Name:

Ask Eric Mathematics Gopher

URL:

gopher://ericir.syr.edu:70/11/Lesson/Subject/Math

Description of Site:

This gopher has been around since before the Internet's current popularity explosion. It is full of lesson plans designed to help you teach math.

What to Do There:

You will notice that gophers are not as pretty as World Wide Web pages. This does not mean that they don't hold a wealth of information. In fact, they tend to be much faster to load and print because of the lack of graphics. Folder icons represent directories of information that may include many documents. Click a folder to view its contents or click a document to view it. Click your print button to print a document.

Name:

Puzzle Junction

URL:

http://web.wwa.com/~stan/puzzles/PuzzleJunction.html

Description of Site:

A place chock-full of quality puzzles and competitions for your enjoyment. Some of the topics include Word Puzzles, Chess Puzzles, Number Puzzles, Brainteasers, and Trivia.

What to Do There:

Kids love puzzles. They challenge the mind and delight the heart. This site houses puzzles of many kinds. Go to the puzzle place and print puzzle pages for use in class or at home. The brain teasers and number puzzles make good warm-up exercises before math.

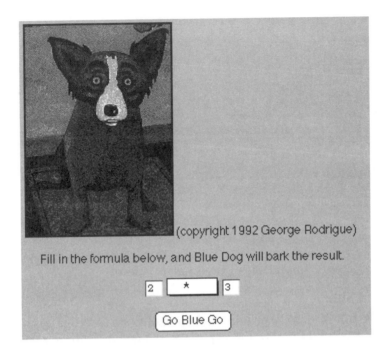

(copyright 1992 George Rodrigue)

Fill in the formula below, and Blue Dog will bark the result.

| 2 | * | 3 |

Go Blue Go

Name:
Blue Dog Can Count

URL:
http://www.forbesfield.com/bdf.html

Description of Site:
Believe it or not, this page is one of the most popular on the Internet. George Rodrique's Blue Dog performs the arithmetic and then answers the question by barking.

What to Do There:
Have younger kids go there to practice their math facts or have them just go there to see some of the capabilities of the Internet.

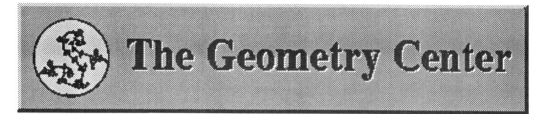

Name:

The Geometry Center

URL:

http://www.geom.umn.edu/

Description of Site:

The Geometry Center is a mathematics research and education center at the University of Minnesota. It was funded by the National Science Foundation as part of the Science and Technology Center program. The Center has a unified mathematics-computing environment supporting math and computer science research, mathematical visualization, software development, application development, video animation production, and K–12 math education.

What to Do There:

What a site! Using some of the most advanced technology on the Internet, this site treats users to visualizations of geometric concepts. They use the advanced technology to create the visualizations, all you need is your web browser and a free finger to click your mouse. Just click the hypertext for Interactive Web Applications and choose a visualization.

Name:

Celebrating Our Nation's Diversity

URL:

http://www.census.gov/ftp/pub/edu/diversity/

Description of Site:

The United States Census Bureau designed this teaching supplement to help teach students about our country's diversity. This teaching tool reinforces these ideas with statistical information, gathered from the 1990 Census of Population and Housing. Also, they have tried to use objectives that fit into the national education goals, which call for students to work with real world data. For example, the National Council of Teachers of Mathematics Standards of Curriculum and Evaluation (NCTM) were used throughout this teaching supplement. It is divided into units for both Elementary and Junior/Senior high school.

What to Do There:

This site is delightfully specific. Use the hypertext link "Dear Educator" to get an overview and then read the background information from which the unit was developed in "Our Diverse Nation." You can get a list of the materials you need by clicking "Bookbag of Materials Needed for These Lessons." Then print out the lessons appropriate to your grade level in "Elementary Edition" or "Junior/Senior High Edition."

Name:

National Geographic Online

URL:

http://www.nationalgeographic.com/

Description of Site:

This site is as wonderful and diverse as any of the National Geographic Society's other media. Travel to other lands, space, or under the ocean. They offer World Magazine for Kids online.

What to Do There:

Where do we start? Anywhere! This is just another great site in which to browse around. If you are looking for specific information on science or social studies, click the Index icon or the Contents to narrow your search to specific stories. This is a perfect place to collect high quality media for use in students' projects. Remember to name your source.

Name:

The National School Weather Network

URL:

http://www.aws.com/

Description of Site:

The Nationwide School Weather Network is a system whereby students record weather information and transmit it to schools all over the United States. This, in addition to real time satellite images, allows students to closely study the data they collect.

What to Do There:

Become a national school weather site. Students involved with this program collect data from a weather station that they put together and report the data back to the network. They then view their results, as well as those from all over the country, along with up-to-date satellite images to make comparisons between the two.

Adventure Online

Name:

Adventure Online

URL:

http://www.adventureonline.com

Description of Site:

Adventure Online is dedicated to bringing adventure and adventure learning to K–12 classrooms and Internet explorers. Serving as a guide to adventure related projects, Adventure Online features exclusive expeditions, adventure news, and entertaining games, as well as developing educational expeditions and adventures. Adventure Online also highlights other projects of educational significance.

What to Do There:

Students can take part virtually in several adventures with explorers from around the world. The geography scavenger hunt game, which features unnamed photos from different parts of the world is particularly good. Weekly clues are given to evoke the sleuth in all of us. Participants must e-mail their responses and winners are awarded wonderful gifts.

RiverResource

Name:

RiverResource

URL:

http://riverresource.com

Description of Site:

RiverResource is a place where students can explore valuable river resources—a gateway to productive Internet exploration. At RiverResource you will not find the facts, but rather the connections to facts, books, and people studying rivers. Here classrooms can share the information they are gathering about rivers.

What to Do There:

Do you teach or live in a city that depends on a river? Historically, geographically, and scientifically, rivers are the life blood of the world. Log-on to this Web site and you will find information about nearly every river in the world. Study a river in your community and share that information with the developers of this site. They will publish your information and even connect you with other classrooms all over the world that are studying rivers.

𝔗𝔥𝔢 𝔖𝔢𝔟𝔢𝔫 𝔚𝔬𝔫𝔡𝔢𝔯𝔰 𝔬𝔣 𝔱𝔥𝔢 𝔄𝔫𝔠𝔦𝔢𝔫𝔱 𝔚𝔬𝔯𝔩𝔡

Name:

The Seven Wonders of the Ancient World

URL:

http://pharos.bu.edu/Egypt/Wonders/

Description of Site:

This site is designed to give users an understanding of the Seven Wonders of the Ancient World.

What to Do There:

This site is a great place to give students historical perspective. For example, if you are studying Egypt and the Great Pyramids, have your students use this site to learn about the building of the Great Pyramid at Giza. Have them then compare this feat with that of the builders of the other six wonders of the world.

Name:
Mapmaker, Mapmaker, Make Me a Map

URL:
http://loki.ur.utk.edu/ut2kids/maps/map.html

Description of Site:
Describes the process of making a map with an interactive glossary of terms.

What to Do There:
Have your students log-on to this site and read through the author's process of making a map. Then have your students log-on to the US Geological Survey site at http://info.er.usgs.gov and view some of the satellite images of different parts of the world. Have them then try to make a map of the area. Ask them how hard it would have been for early explorers to map the world.

USA CITYLINK

Name:

USA CityLink

URL:

http://www.usacitylink.com

Description of Site:

The USA CityLink Project is the most comprehensive United States city and state listing on the Web, as well as one of the most visited sites on the Internet today. It provides users with a starting point when accessing information about U.S. states and cities.

What to Do There:

This is a good place to start when looking for information for state and city reports. A good activity to teach students how to navigate the net is to send them on a virtual tour. Give them a list of cities to visit and have them start with City Net. They can move from city to city and collect something from each city they visit.

Name:

The Whitehouse Home Page

URL:

http://www.whitehouse.gov/

Description of Site:

This Web site is maintained by the Office of the President of the United States and contains information about the first family and the executive branch.

What to Do There:

Take a virtual tour of the White House. You can do this by clicking the "Tour" button on the page. E-mail the President or Vice President a letter convincing them to support or not support some current legislation. Collect media for a report or presentation on the First Family. With a Web browser such as Netscape you simply click the picture you want and save it. Research the Executive Branch of government by simply clicking the button on the home page and getting a complete description of the duties of the Office of the President.

Name:

The Library of Congress

URL:

http://www.loc.gov/

Description of Site:

The Library of Congress presents information about and materials from its collections over the Internet. Its online information and services include the following: schedules of exhibits and events, a menu of services provided, a substantial digital library of various text and media, an online catalog system, information on Congress and the government, as well as links to related WWW sites.

What to Do There:

Research the branches of government by searching for information about our political system. Collect media for presentations by pointing and clicking on the media desired. Get e-mail addresses of the members of Congress and write them about important issues. You pay for it, you might as well use it.

Name:
Virtual Tourist

URL:
http://www.vtourist.com

Description of Site:
The Virtual Tourist is an electronic map of the world, with each section consisting of a hypermedia link of general information and thousands of pictures of places all over the world.

What to Do There:
Use the media collected from this site to make pamphlets advertising places all over the world. Play an online geography scavenger hunt. Have students collect pictures and text about different countries that you assign. E-mail tourist information offices in different countries requesting information.

 Virtual Library  World museums Search Culture

M useums

Name:

Virtual Museums

URL:

http://www.comlab.ox.ac.uk/archive/other/museums.html

Description of Site:

These pages provide an eclectic collection of WWW services connected with museums, galleries, and archives.

What to Do There:

Use this site as a starting point from which to search for social studies information that might be included in a museum. Surf around to the different museums keeping in mind your curriculum and what each museum has to offer. Make bookmarks for sites that are of interest and useful for you or your students.

classroom
CONNECT

GalapagosQuest

Join us on March 1, 1999 as the team heads for the tiny Galapagos Islands off the coast of Ecuador. You can direct our team as they scuba and sail through these enchanted isles.

Subscribe to GalapagosQuest
Purchase your curriculum package.

See pages from our Curriculum Guide
Use Adobe Acrobat to view a sample lesson.

Preview the Web site schedule
Find out about the daily features and activities

Experience a Quest
Relive one of our past adventures

Find out about future Quests
Travel with the team to Asia and the

Name:

Classroom Connect's Quests

URL:

http://quest.classroom.com

Description of Site:

In the spring of 1995, a team of five explorers, led by Dan Buettner, bicycled to ruins in Mexico and Central America, met with on-site archaeologists, and attempted to unlock one of the most perplexing mysteries of the modern era: the collapse of the ancient Maya civilization. The team was not alone however, over one-million kids, teachers, and others from around the globe helped to lead the expedition by way of the Internet. Now Classroom Connect has expanded this project by offering Quests to different areas of the world like Asia, Africa, and the Galapagos Islands.

What to Do There:

Take part in the activity by registering or just observe what is going on and use the resources that the scientists leave for you here. Either way your class will feel as if they are involved in this virtual field trip.

Name:
MapQuest

URL:
http://www.mapquest.com/

Description of Site:
MapQuest is an interactive mapping service that includes two parts. Interactive Atlas allows you to find any place in the world. Just click on the postcards to begin your MapQuest. TripQuest provides city to city driving directions for the United States, and parts of Canada and Mexico.

What to Do There:
Use the Interactive atlas to do research about the geography of any part of the world. Collect maps for reports or simply the site to learn about geography. Use the TripQuest section for integrated math/geography projects. Have your students plan a route to travel and estimate time and distance using scale and distance per hour.

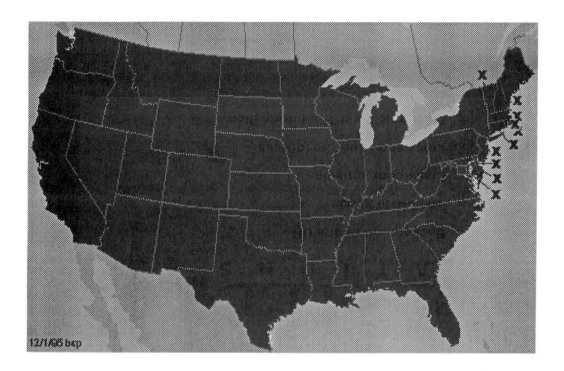

Name:

Do You Know Your State Capitals?

URL:

http://www.cris.com/~Kraft/capitals/

Description of Site:

This is a neat little site to have students test and practice their knowledge of states and capitals. Great for homework.

What to Do There:

Have your students log-on from home or school. They first click the state they want to guess, then they name the state and its capital. The site returns feedback if the student is wrong.

Name:

Electronic Field Trip to the United Nations

URL:

http://www.pbs.org/tal/un/

Description of Site:

This Web site was produced as part of the 1995–96 electronic field trip series by the Public Broadcasting Service and Turner Adventure Learning. Although the broadcast and print components are no longer available, this Web site has numerous resources that can complement your studies.

What to Do There:

Although you cannot take part in this project anymore, the activities and background information are fantastic. Browse through the activities during an International Week celebration or use it to do a unit on the United Nations.

Name:

History/Social Studies Web Site for K-12 Teachers

URL:

http://execpc.com/~dboals/boals.html

Description of Site:

The major purpose of this home page is to begin the task of making use of the Internet for busy social studies teachers and to encourage the use of the World Wide Web as a tool for learning and teaching. The documents, links, and text files listed in the various categories should provide some help for classroom teachers in locating and using the resources of the Internet in the classroom.

What to Do There:

Browse to find Web sites that can help you enhance your social studies curriculum and teaching.

World Wide Holidays and Events

Name:
World Wide Holidays and Events

URL:
http://www.classnet.com/holidays/

Description of Site:
World Wide Holidays and Events is an interactive calendar that references 198 countries and 470 holidays. The calendar includes information about holidays and counties that celebrate them.

What to Do There:
If you are looking for information about holidays and how different countries celebrate them, this is a great place to start. This search engine allows you to search by date, country, or event. Log on daily to see what holidays are being celebrated in different countries in the "Today Holidays" area. Have students compare how and if other countries celebrate some of the holidays that they celebrate by searching the event in all countries.

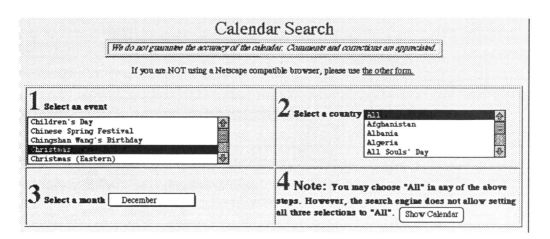

Name:

NativeWeb Resources

URL:

http://www.nativeweb.org/resources

Description of Site:

An extensive listing of resources for Indigenous people around the world.

What to Do There:

If you teach a unit on Native Americans, this is a must see. Of particular interest to teachers and students are the searchable databases of the following:

- Arts & Humanities
- Historical Material
- Languages & Linguistics
- Libraries & Collections
- Nations Web Sites & Information
- Reference Materials
- Society & Culture

AMERICAN MEMORY

Name:

American Memory Library of Congress

URL:

http://www.loc.gov

Description of Site:

At the Learning Page of the Library of Congress, you will find the Pathfinder indexes that guide you through the American Memory historical collections and other Library of Congress resources. This is an excellent source for classroom ideas and professional resources.

What to Do There:

You can use this site as a starting point for researching American history. There are several entries in the digital library to browse though. Check the activities section to find the History Mysteries. A perfect activity for teaching researching skills, History Mysteries poses a question about a historic event, then gives clues to follow through the vast resources of the Library of Congress Online to solve the mystery.

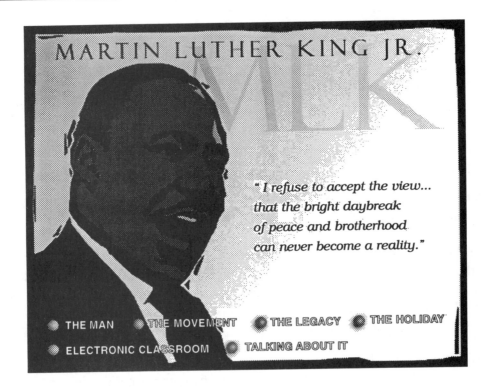

Name:

The Seattle Times' Martin Luther King Online Edition

URL:

http://www.seattletimes.com/mlk/

Description of Site:

This site deals with the history of the man and the movement. The site has a special focus on the Pacific Northwest, but it also reaches across the country, establishing an electronic dialog between school children in Birmingham and in the Seattle area. You will visit the scenes of the civil rights past and hear the voices of some of those contemplating the future.

What to Do There:

Use this site as a resource for information about Martin Luther King and the Civil Rights Movement. After covering the content, have students take the interactive quiz to test their knowledge.

The National Budget Simulation

Name:

National Budget Simulation

URL:

http://garnet.berkeley.edu:3333/budget/budget.html

Description of Site:

This simulation asks you to cut the 1995 fiscal deficit in order to achieve a balanced budget. In order to make the choices we face in the budget clearer, we assume that you make the cuts all in one year. You may also want to increase spending in areas that you think are being shortchanged under present budget priorities.

What to Do There:

This project should be used with students of not less than seventh grade. Students are asked to increase or decrease certain areas of government spending. Discuss what each section is and the possible impact of their actions. Have them decide on an action. Use the menus to make budget cuts. The browser will return with the amount that they had cut or increased the deficit. If nothing else, this simulation teaches your students how complex the decisions are.

Name:
The CIA World Factbook

URL:
http://www.odci.gov/cia/publications/factbook/index.html

Description of Site:
Who better to give you the inside scoop on the world but the Central Intelligence Agency. This is an index of every country in the world and the major facts about it. Each country page is laid out in identical format, starting with maps of the country and ending with a surprising amount of information.

What to Do There:
The perfect place to get information for country reports. Assign students a country then have them surf to this site, print out country information, and save maps on a disk for use in the final report. Compare statistics like infant mortality and longevity of life from one country to another to make generalizations about regions.

Name:

GlobaLearn

URL:

http://www.globalearn.org/

Description of Site:

Join GlobaLearn and thousands of school children for an expedition to thrilling places around the world. Embark on the journey via the Internet. Follow four GlobaLearn explorers and a support crew as they retrace the same steps that early explorers once used.

What to Do There:

Register and follow the expedition through daily reports from the team. Communicate with the team or other classes via an electronic bulletin board. Collect pictures from the gallery, where the explorers post pictures of what they are seeing. Use the archived collection of records from past expeditions to learn about other adventures.

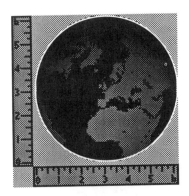

Name:
How Far Is It?

URL:
http://www.indo.com/distance/

Description of Site:
This service uses the University of Michigan Geographic Name Server and a supplementary database of world cities to find the latitude and longitude of two places, and then calculates the distance between them (i.e., as the crow flies or in a straight line). It also provides a map showing the two places.

What to Do There:
If you are teaching longitude and latitude or relative distance, this site is a super supplement. You or your students simply enter the names of the two places that you are interested in. The computer comes back with the longitude and latitude and distance between the two sites. Have students estimate the distances and longitude/latitude before looking them up. Then log on and compare their estimates to the actual results.

GENEALOGY

Name:

GENEALOGY

URL:

http://www.execpc.com/~dboals/geneo.html

Description of Site:

This site offers a whole lot of resources that can help K–12 students research their family histories. As the author says, collecting data, obtaining and evaluating documents and sources, and conducting and recording eyewitness accounts of historical events in family life provide opportunities to practice the historians craft. We should ask student/historians to weed and cull, to evaluate, to interpret, and to assign value to historical events and accounts of those events.

What to Do There:

Have students explore the "Select Family Web Sites" and browse through a few to introduce them to genealogy research. Have them then begin to create a family tree. You might also want your students to interview grandparents to get an oral history before starting. Use the tips on how to begin, located in the General Resources section of this site.

K-12 Electronic Guide for African Resources on the Internet

Name:

K–12 Electronic Guide for African Resources on the Internet

URL:

http://www.sas.upenn.edu/African_Studies/Home_Page/AFR_GIDE.html

Description of Site:

The aim of this guide is to assist K–12 teachers, librarians, and students in locating online resources on Africa that can be used in the classroom, for research and studies.

What to Do There:

Looking for resources about the diverse African nations? Use this site as a starting point for students who are studying Africa. Some of the resources include lesson plans, media libraries, and connections to other students in African countries.

Postcard Geography

Name:

Postcard Geography

URL:

http://www.internet-catalyst.org

Description of Site:

This project is being offered to classes all over the world via the Internet, be prepared to receive and send hundreds of cards. It is appropriate for all ages and will run in two sessions: August through December and January through May. Each session will require separate registration. In this simple project, your class commits to exchanging picture postcards (purchased or computer/handmade) with all other participating classes.

What to Do There:

This is one of the most exciting yet simple classroom connecting projects on the Internet. Simply log on to this site and register for the project by filling in the registration form. After registration closes, you can download a list of participating classes (usually in the hundreds) and use the list to print mailing labels. Have your students buy or make postcards that highlight your area or community and send them to the participants. Soon the postcards from other classes around the world will begin to trickle in. Make a bulletin board of a map of the world and put your postcards up. Have students report on the areas from which you receive postcards. Write back to classes that send you cards.

The 50 States of the United States
Their Capital Cities and Information Links

Name:

The 50 States

URL:

http://www.scvol.com/States/main.htm

Description of Site:

This site is arranged into information links for all 50 states. Use the image map of the United States or simply click the link of the state's name to find a wealth of information for each.

What to Do There:

This is the perfect site to start with when doing reports on a particular state. Have students explore several states while looking for one to be the subject of their report. Once they have chosen, assign several areas for them to research. Make sure to have them collect pictures or media for reports, as well as presentations.

Name:

AskAsia

URL:

http://www.askasia.org/

Description of Site:

AskAsia makes teaching and learning about Asia—from culture to politics, from history to religion—as easy as NIKO NIKO (that's Japanese for smiling happily). Developed by The Asia Society in cooperation with several partners, AskAsia offers high quality, carefully selected resources to steer both the novice and the veteran.

What to Do There:

Take a virtual trip to Asia. There are several teacher lesson plans, as well as many pieces of media. Have students visit the For Kids Only section to experience the Asian cultures through kid's eyes.

Name:

The Multicultural Book Review

URL:

http://www.isomedia.com/homes/jmele/homepage.html

Description of Site:

The purpose of this page is to create a qualitative list of multicultural literature for K–12 educators. MBR would like to avoid presenting just lists of books, but would instead like to give educators a chance to find out a little more information about multicultural literature others have used successfully.

What to Do There:

This web site reviews multicultural books by and for teachers. To find a book choose Reviews. Then choose the type of cultural material which you are looking for. The site includes the following: African-American Literature, Asian-American/Pacific Islander Literature, Latino and Latina Literature, Native American and Eskimo Literature, Jewish Literature, Middle Eastern and East Indian Literature, Titles in English from Other Countries, Textbooks, and Multiple Ethnicities. To submit a book just choose Submit a Book and follow the directions.

The Quotations Page

Name:
The Quotations Page

URL:
http://www.starlingtech.com/quotes/about.html

Description of Site:
This site catalogues thousands of quotations. You can search for a quote by keywords or simply browse through the list of quotations.

What to Do There:
Clicking the search button and entering a keyword gets you a list of quotations. After entering the word "teach," the site returned with seven quotes from one location, one of which was these words of wisdom: "Quite frankly, teachers are the only profession that teach our children." Vice President Dan Quayle, 9/18/90. Have students find quotations about things that interest them, like "playing" or "games" and then have them interpret what the author meant.

Carrie's Sites for Educators

Name:

Carrie's Sites for Educators

URL:

http://www.mtjeff.com/~bodenst/page5.html

Description of Site:

Carrie compiles a very comprehensive site of hypertext links to teacher resources. Her site is divided into the following: Search Engines, Oregon Resources, General Educational Resources, Counseling and Guidance Resources, Humanities Resources, Social Studies Resources, Science Resources, Math Resources, Internet in the Classroom Resources, Vocational Resources, and Technical Resources.

What to Do There:

A great starting place for searches of educational resources. Check out the Internet in the Classroom link to find out how you can use the Internet more efficiently and creatively.

The Complete Works
of
William Shakespeare

Name:

The Complete Works of William Shakespeare

URL:

http://the-tech.mit.edu/Shakespeare/works.html

Description of Site:

William Shakepeare's works are catalogued and sorted in several ways. The complete text of each play is available in a hyperdocument. This means that several of the words and phrases are able to be clicked on in order to annotate with descriptions and definitions.

What to Do There:

Have your students use this site to study the works of Shakespeare. Teach literary skills such as similes and metaphors, then have your students read through one of the works in search of examples. Hypertext will allow them to get explanations so that they can interpret the text easier.

the poetry corner

Name:

the poetry corner

URL:

http://pluto.njcc.com/~begun/welcome.html

Description of Site:

This site is dedicated to the publishing of poets of all ages. It seeks to provide a database of contributed poetry. Poems are displayed for all to enjoy.

What to Do There:

Have students read and comment on poetry at this sight. Send e-mail to the authors to ask questions. You can even submit poetry that your students have written.

Name:

enews

URL:

http://www.enews.com/

Description of Site:

The Electronic Newsstand is the Web's premiere magazine site. Founded in 1993, it was also one of the first content based sites on the Internet. This site contains the largest and most diverse magazine related resources anywhere on the Web. The Newsstand is home to more than 200 actual magazine sites.

What to Do There:

This is a great place to get up to the minute news on just about any topic. Have students log on and print an article to read and report on for current events or have them compare and contrast this electronic medium with the more traditional magazine media. What are the plusses and minuses of both?

The Giraffe Project

Stick Your Neck Out

Name:

The Giraffe Project

URL:

http://www.whidbey.com/giraffe/

Description of Site:

This groups' goal is to find, commend, and publicize people who stick their necks out for the common good. Their mission is to get others to follow their lead. They are also the source of The Giraffe Program, a K–12 curriculum that teaches kids about real heroes and gets them going on lives of courage, caring, and responsibility.

What to Do There:

"Students lack quality role models" is a familiar refrain these days. This site tells the stories of people who stick their necks out and get involved. Use The Giraffe Program for Kids to help teach and foster values in the classroom. Kids can even nominate their own Giraffes.

Carol Hurst's Children's Literature Site
by Carol Otis Hurst and Rebecca Otis

Name:

Carol Hurst's Children's Literature Site

URL:

http://www.carolhurst.com/

Description of Site:

This is a collection of reviews of great books for kids, ideas of ways to use them in the classroom, and collections of books and activities about particular subjects, curriculum areas, themes and professional topics. They have taken many of Carol Hurst's back articles and sections from her professional books for teachers and librarians and reformatted and interlinked them to create an interactive collection of information.

What to Do There:

If you are interested in how to integrate literature into Math, Social Studies, and the other content areas this is a great place for resources. Thematic guides are also available so that teachers can make connections with the literature within themes used in the classroom. Each subject contains children's book titles, activities, links to related areas of this site and links to other sites on the Internet.

Ken Fansler's Online
Instruction Page

Name:

Ken Fansler's Online Music Instruction Page

URL:

http://orathost.cfa.ilstu.edu/public/KenFansler/onlinemusicpage.htm

Description of Site:

The Online Music Instruction home page is designed to teach you some of the basics of music theory and give you an opportunity to test your knowledge of music. The three levels of skill are as follows: beginner, intermediate, and advanced. It is recommended that you start at the beginner level and move up to the higher levels as you feel comfortable.

What to Do There:

Use the site as a weekly music lesson for your students. Each level is divided into lessons complete with pictures and sounds. When each student completes a section, there is even a test to check for understanding. If you cannot have kids online, just print out the lessons and save the sounds and pictures to your computer. Display these on an overhead or other large screen projection device.

Name:

ArtServe

URL:

http://rubens.anu.edu.au/

Description of Site:

This server, in the Department of Art History at the Australian National University, offers access to approximately 18,500 images (i.e., some 3.8Gb of data) all concerned in some way with the history of art and architecture. (This information is NOT available anywhere else.)

What to Do There:

This is a searchable database of art history. Have students search for a specific time period or artist. Have them compare and contrast styles and/or time periods. Have them evaluate the artist's style.

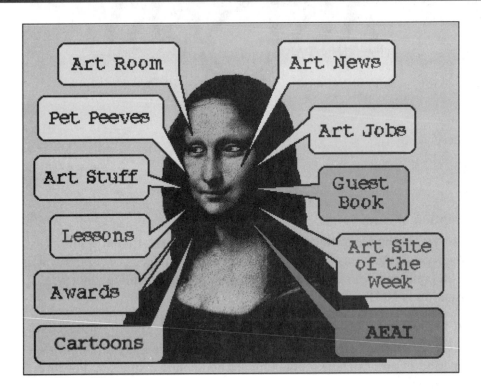

Name:

The Incredible Art Department

URL:

http://Artswire.org/Kenroar/index.html

Description of Site:

This site includes an Art Room that displays art, Art News, Art Stuff, Lessons, Cartoons, Best of the Net, Guest Book, Awards, and Art Site of the Week.

What to Do There:

Use this site as a basis for your art program. Whether you are teaching art history, style, appreciation, or technique, this site has what you need. Go to the Art Lessons sections for lesson plans from teachers all over the web. Do you have a lesson that works? Submit it for others to use.

Name:

ArtsEdNet

URL:

http://www.artsednet.getty.edu/

Description of Site:

ArtsEdNet, is an online service developed by the Getty Education Institute for the Arts, it supports the needs of the K–12 arts education community. It focuses on helping art educators, general classroom teachers using the arts in their curriculum, museum educators, and university faculty involved in the arts.

What to Do There:

If you are an art teacher follow the Teacher Resource link to Lesson Plans, there you will find discipline based activities. If you are interested in integrating art into your curriculum try the Curriculum Ideas link for a more open-ended way of teaching the disciplines of art.

Name:

ArtsEdge

URL:

http://artsedge.kennedy-center.org/artsedge.html

Description of Site:

The mission of ArtsEdge is to help artists, teachers, and students gain access to and/or share information, resources, and ideas that support the arts as a core subject area in the K–12 curriculum. To do this, ArtsEdge provides information and resources divided into the following areas: NewsBreak, Community Center, Web Spotlight, Search Lab, Curriculum Studio, and For Students.

What to Do There:

Browse the areas until you get a feel for what integrating art into the curriculum means. Then go to the curriculum studio and look for lesson plans and resources that can enhance your curriculum. Pick the subject area you would like to integrate art into by clicking the hypertext to which it corresponds.

Name:

@URL Internet Arts Resources: Dance

URL:

http://url.co.nz/arts/dance.html

Description of Site:

This hotlist makes links to a representative sample of dance resources on the World Wide Web.

What to Do There:

Although this site has pointers to information on almost any type of dance, the Folk Dance and History of Dance sections are of the most value to educators. Use this site in conjunction with a unit of study on countries or cultures of the world. You might also look at the Virtual Tourist web site (page 212) in order to round out the resources needed for this type of unit.

GLOSSARY

Address (electronic mail address or Internet address)—An electronic mail or e-mail address is the group of characters that you must give an electronic mail program to direct a message to a person. An Internet address is the set of numbers assigned to a computer on the Internet (e.g., 204.23.456.78.98).

.aiff—This is a sound file format.

Archie—This is a method of searching for files on FTP servers.

.au—This is a sound file format.

Bits Per Second (bps)—This is a measure of data transmission speed.

Baud—This is a term associated with the speed of modems.

BIT (Binary DigIT)—This is the smallest amount of information which may be stored in a computer.

Browser—This is software that you use to view html-pages. Well known browsers are *Netscape, Internet Explorer*, and *Mosaic*.

Bulletin Board System (BBS)—This is a place where you can post electronic messages.

By the Way (BTW)—This is an abbreviation used in newsgroups, chat, and e-mail.

Byte—This is one character of information, usually eight bits wide.

Dedicated Line—It is a permanently connected private telephone line between two locations.

Domain Name Server (DNS)—This is a server that associates names (e.g., eric.org) with the computer, with the Internet address that corresponds to the name.

Download—This is to transfer files from one computer to another.

E-mail—This is short for electronic mail.

File Transfer Protocol (FTP)—This is a method of transferring files to and from remote computers.

For Sale (FS)—An abbreviation in newsgroups, chat, and e-mail.

Frequently Asked Questions (FAQs)—This is a text document containing a collection of frequently asked questions pertaining to a certain topic.

Graphics Interchange Format (GIF)—This is an image file format.

Gigabyte (GB or Gig)—This is a unit of data storage size which represents one billion characters of information.

Gopher—This is a text based information system developed at the University of Minnesota.

GLOSSARY *(cont.)*

Home Page—This is a top (menu) level document of an organization, or a document that a user frequently visits.

Hotlist—These are sites that you visit frequently on the Internet.

Hypertext Markup Language (html)—These are the rules that control the way Web documents are created so that they can be read by a WWW browser.

Hypertext Transport Protocol (http)—This is the protocol used by the WWW servers.

Hyperlink—This is a link from one document to another. These links are usually represented by highlighted and/or underlined words or images that can be clicked.

Hypermedia—These are documents containing a variety of media types, such as text, images, movies, and audio.

In My Opinion (IMO)—An abbreviation used in newsgroups, chat, and e-mail.

In My Humble Opinion (IMHO)—An abbreviation used in newsgroups, chat, and e-mail.

I/O—Input/Output

In-line Image—This is a graphic image that is displayed within an html document.

Internet—This is an international network of connected computer networks.

Internet Protocol (IP)—This is the basic way that data is exchanged on the Internet.

Joint Photographic Expert Group (JPEG)—This is a method of storing an image in digital format.

Kilobyte (KB)—This is a unit of data storage size which represents 1,024 characters of information.

Local Area Network (LAN)—This is a network of computers in proximity to one another.

MacTCP—This is the network software from Apple Computer that allows Macintosh to interact with the other computers.

Megabyte (MB or Meg)—This is a unit of data storage (one million characters of information).

Multipurpose Internet Mail Extensions (MIME)—It tags e-mail to keep it from being changed as they move throughout the Internet.

GLOSSARY *(cont.)*

Modem—This is a piece of equipment that connects a computer to a data transmission line (typically a telephone line).

Moving Pictures Experts Group (MPEG)—This is a way of storing movie files in digital format.

NCSA—The National Center for Supercomputing Applications

Network News Transfer Protocol (NNTP)—This is the way that Newsgroups are transferred.

Point-to-Point Protocol (PPP)—This is a way to connect your computer to the Internet.

Protocol—This is a planned method of exchanging data over the Internet.

QuickTime—This is a method of storing movie and audio files in a digital format. It was developed by Apple Computer.

Reply (Re:)—This is a common abbreviation in news-groups used to indicate that this mail is a response to a previous one.

Rolling on the Floor Laughing (ROTFL)—This is an abbreviation used in newsgroups, chat, and e-mail.

Serial Line Internet Protocol (SLIP)—This is a way to connect your computer to the Internet.

Server—This is a computer that serves information and software to the Internet.

Simple Mail Transfer Protocol (SMTP)—This is the current method of how most of today's e-mail is transferred from computer to computer.

Tag Image File Format (TIFF)—This is a file format used to store image files.

Transmission Control Protocol/Internet Protocol (TCP/IP)—This is a set of rules that are followed for transmitting data over the Internet.

Uniform Resource Locator (URL)—This is an address to a source of information on the Internet (e.g., http://www.teachercreated.com)

Users Network (USENET)—This is the source of all newsgroups.

Veronica—This is software that searches for filenames on Gopher servers.

Wanted to Buy (WTB)—This is an abbreviation used in newsgroups, chat, and e-mail.

WAN—Wide Area Network

Wide Area Information Server (WAIS)—This is a database.

World Wide Web (WWW or The Web)—This is a system of html-pages which are interconnected via hyperlinks.

Technology Funding and Donations

Contrary to popular belief, the most common question asked concerning educational technology is not "How do I turn the thing on?" but the more serious question of "How do we pay for all of this?" With shrinking school budgets and the increasing demand for current innovation in the classroom, how can schools keep up? There are resources available for teachers and schools, and it is quite frequently just a matter of expressing a need, submitting an application, and formulating a technology plan. The following is a list of foundations, coalitions, technology educational funds, and the like which offer financial assistance to schools seeking technology.

1. **Foundation Center** has published a directory listing over 6,000 large foundations which donated over $9 billion dollars last year. This publication is called *The Foundation Directory*. It includes descriptions of grants, fundraising examples, and grant makers' priorities in addition to listings of these foundations. The cost is $195 for hardcover and $170 for softcover. There are other helpful publications available as well.

   Contact: The Foundation Center
   Dept. PR35
   79 Fifth Avenue
   New York, NY 10003-3076
   (800) 424-9836

2. The **U.S. Department of Education** offers a listing of national educational technology groups and other resources through its Goals 2000 Resource Center. For more information call (800) USA-LEARN.

   Also from the U.S. Department of Education is an annual listing of grants and fellowships offered by various offices of education. There are a variety of deadlines, levels of support, and eligibility requirements. The publication, *The Federal Register*, cost is $4.50.

   Contact: Superintendent of Documents
   U.S. Government Printing Office
   Washington, D.C. 20402

TECHNOLOGY FUNDING AND DONATIONS *(cont.)*

3. **CompuMentor** is a nonprofit group which offers corporation-donated software and computer books at low cost to nonprofit groups and schools. DOS software is $25 and MAC is $6.

> Contact: CompuMentor
> 89 Stillman Street
> San Francisco, CA 94107

4. **The Software Publishers Association** and **Gifts in Kind America** are working together to collect donations of software for schools and nonprofit organizations nationwide. 1n 1993 over $16 million dollars worth of software was donated by groups such as Microsoft, Lotus, Egghead, Claris, Aldus, and WordPerfect.

> Contact: Gifts in Kind America
> 700 North Fairfax Street #300
> Alexandria, VA 22314

TECHNOLOGY FUNDING AND DONATIONS *(cont.)*

◆ Foundation Directories

Foundation Reporter
Corporate Giving Directory
(800) 877-8238

The Foundation Grants Index
(800) 424-9836

Directory of Major State Foundations
Logos Associates
P.O. Box 31
Woodsville, NH 03785-0031

◆ Finding Up-to-Date Federal Information

Education Funding Research Council
Federal Opportunities Books and Newsletters
(800) 876-0226

Capitol Publishers
Education and Foundation Grants Information
(800) 221-0425

INDEX

INDEX *(cont.)*

INDEX *(cont.)*

INDEX *(cont.)*

BIBLIOGRAPHY

Print Resources

Butler, Mark. *How to Use the Internet.* Ziff-Davis Press, 1994.

Giagnocavo, Gregory, Tim McLain, and Vince DiStefano. *Educator's Internet Companion.* Wentworth Worldwide Media, Inc., 1995.

Haag, Tim. *Internet For Kids.* Teacher Created Materials, 1996.

James, Phil. *Netscape Navigator 2.0 Book: The Definitive Guide to the World's Most Popular Internet Navigator.* Ventana Communications Group, 1996.

Lichty, Tom. *The Official America Online for the Macintosh Tour: 2nd Edition.* Ventana Press, 1994.

McLain, Tim and Vince DiStefano. *Educator's Worldwide Web Tour Guide.* Wentworth World-wide Media, Inc., 1995.

Periera, Linda. *Computers Don't Byte.* Teacher Created Materials, 1996.

Online Resources

Heitkötter, Jörg. *The Big Dummy's Guide to the Internet* [Online]. The Electronic Frontier Foundation's, 1993. Available: http://wwwpc.hrz.th-darmstadt.de/bdgtti/bdg_1.htm

Anonymous. *NCSA Beginner's Guide to HTML* [Online]. The National Center for Supercomputing Applications, 1996. Available:
http://www.ncsa.uiuc.edu/General/Internet/WWW/HTMLPrimer.html

Hixson, Susan. *Internet in the Classroom* [Online]. 1996. Available:
http://www.indirect.com/www/dhixson/class.html

Lin, Larry. *Creating a Successful Web Page* [Online]. Available:
http://www.hooked.net/~larrylin/web.htm

Collins, Stephen E. *Web66: A K12 World Wide Web Project* [Online]. Web66
1996. Available: http://web66.coled.umn.edu/

Anonymous. *Internet and Web Help.* Earthlink Network, 1996. Available:
http://www.earthlink.net/nethelp/

Anonymous. *21st Century Teachers.* 21st Century Teacher's Organization,
1996. Available: http://www.21ct.org/

Anonymous. *Acceptable Use Policies, 1995.* Available:
http://www.nmusd.k12.ca.us/Resources/Policies.html

Steve Davidson. *Back to School: Looking to the New Millennium, September 1996.* Available: http://www.teleport.com/~stdavid/sjintro.html